OVERCOMER

A HEARTFELT JOURNEY OF ONE WOMAN'S FIGHT TO OVERCOME BREAST CANCER.

"While waiting for my results, someone whom I respect a great deal called me. After he told me his whole family was praying for me, he made a statement that I held onto during the really tough days. He said, "Denika, when I think of you and how you have fought this fight, I think, "She has the heart of a lion!" (Excerpt from Chapter 18: Surgery: Inside and Out)

DENIKA PHILPOTT

Denika Philpott

OVERCOMER

Copyright © 2016 by Denika Philpott

Softcover ISBN: 978-0-9958001-0-6
Hardcover ISBN: 978-0-9958001-2-0
E-book ISBN: 978-0-9958001-1-3

To order additional copies, visit: https://journeywithdenika.wordpress.com/

Cover photo credit: Darryl Pike
Back cover photo credit: Michele Fraser
About Author photo credit: Wanda (Cooze) Stead
Cover design and interior production by: Vaughan King
Published 2016 by Vahen King Ministries
www.vahenking.com

Cataloguing data available from Library and Archives Canada
Printed in the United States of America

Reflections of my
Family & Friends

Denika, the love of my life, has given me the honor of writing this reflection for her book. This is a book that I have not only read but lived as well. This is no easy task for me as the thoughts of this past year run through my mind as they do on a day to day basis. The tears are running down my face. Denika and my daughter Laura will appreciate the tears.

Denika said to me from the day she was diagnosed with cancer that no one knows what or how she feels going through this journey—this fight for her life. It took me a while to understand what she meant. All I could see was that "my best friend, my lover, my soul mate, my wife" was being taken over by the one thing that I think we all fear the most: the Big C. As much as I could not feel what she was feeling or take the pain away, I was her biggest fighting fan. I just wanted her to beat this. I prayed many a day and night that she would be OK, overcome, and that it would all disappear. All I wanted was to take it all away. In my heart and soul I knew she would beat this. I know Denika. She is a fighter and a lover of life (some of my favorite qualities about her.)

This book started as a journal to keep track of everything going on in her life between doctor appointments, chemo, and different types of scans and tests. It turned into a detailed account of her living with cancer and how she dealt with it. Her fight would amaze even the strongest of "men." (I learned that women are way stronger than men.) Denika is an amazing person who has touched a lot of people's lives over the years; but, never in a million years would I think that this beautiful person who had so much on her plate would prove to be my Hero. I could only imagine me being half the person she is.

As you read her life in this book you will see the struggles, the pain, the heartache, and the fear of leaving her family behind from a disease that only the devil himself could have invented. But here's where my amazing wife, the "Overcomer," puts her amazing touch on it. She decided early in this journey to let the world see inside her fears and her day to day struggles with chemo, radiation, and recovery from surgeries. She did this through social media and talking to what I now call "true friends." She frequently posted a day to day account of what hurdle she had overcome that day. Over the months she would have countless friends and even strangers show up on her door step with anything from a cooked meal, a hug, a prayer, or just a pop-in cup of tea. As the days went by, people and friends would tell her how she was inspiring them. Her strength in a time when most others would be weakened gave them strength to get through their own personal struggles.

I have said this a lot over the past few years: never has one person amazed me so much! And the best part is I get to share my life with her! This gives me the bragging rights of being the luckiest man alive. She makes me ME. Noah summed it all up one morning as he was getting up for school: " Mom, I'm just getting out of bed and you with cancer already have clothes in the washer and got bread baked; you're amazing." Be prepared to meet my amazing wife and how she kicked cancer to the curb. And yes, I could never use enough "amazing's" to describe my life partner. Denika, I love you and life without you is not an option. Hubby XO

PS: I wish I could write as good as I could cry, LOL!!

Darryl Pike
Denika's husband
Torbay, Newfoundland Labrador

* * *

I knew Mom was going to make it through because she's Mom. She has survived many other things, including a black eye from the doorknob, and being run over by a car at a young age. She is a strong and determined woman who isn't planning on leaving Earth anytime soon. Working out and eating healthy has played a part in her survival through cancer. Many of her friends have died of cancer, but she simply said, "Not today" to it and she is almost fully recovered.

Noah Lewis
Denika's son, Age 14

* * *

I kept asking God, "Why?" Why He would do this to a loving, beautiful Mom who worships God. But I realized that everything happens for a reason. I didn't know what that reason was at the time but I knew there must be a good one. My Mom is the strongest person I know.

When Mom first got cancer, all I could think was: nothing. My mind went blank. Then it hit me and the tears started rolling down my face and I panicked. All I could think of was that my Mom might die. I called my friend and gave her the news. She calmed me down a little bit but everything was still a blur.

I didn't know what to do that night. I prayed and again I asked God, "Why?" It took me about two hours to go to sleep that night.

The next thing I knew, my Mom was bald. Her beautiful, colorful hair was gone. Then a few months later she had surgery. When I went to visit her at the hospital, my mind was blank once again. My beautiful Mom was in pain, and I was in pain. I didn't know how to deal with it at the time.

My two friends were there for me the entire time because they knew how I felt. Their Mom was also going through cancer. Every time I felt angry or sad, they gave me a shoulder to cry on.

Now my Mom is a healthy and loving Mom who is cancer-free. I'm no longer scared, sad, or angry. I love you, Mommy.

Abigail Lewis
Denika's daughter, Age 12

* * *

Denika is the youngest of four siblings and I am the oldest. I remember the day she was born. I was so happy to be able to be a "little mommy" to Denika rather than an older sister. Over the years we have been through lots together but we were never really "close" because of the gap in our age.

On Oct 8, 2015, Denika called me and gave me the terrible news: she had cancer! Well, the big sister instinct kicked into overdrive! We have learned so much about each other this past year and I'll tell you, she is one heck of a human being! Her strength and determination blew my mind; and, I realized this cancer was in for one heck of a ride!

A year later Denika has a new lease on life. She has learned what is important and what is not. She's experienced what to hold onto and what to let go of. Today we have a fresh new relationship. It is a friendship that I cherish and love! When you see someone you love at their lowest, there is no hiding who you really are. It all comes out, the good and the bad. But, in the end, you have a relationship that is raw and real and it's awesome! I love you, sister!

Michele Fraser
Denika's oldest sister
Strathmore, Alberta

* * *

Denika suggested I start my reflection with "When I first found out…" I have many moments I remember from the last 18 months of Denika's fight, but "when I found out" is not one of them. I remember the feeling and telling my husband, but not the moment. When you read her story, you will see that the weeks before her diagnosis were such that cancer was a surprise, but not a shock.

Understand that Denika is a wonderful mother, an incredible friend, and a strong person. She is dedicated, smart, kind, and obviously resilient. Supporting her and being in her corner is never hard. Cancer affected every part of her life as she has expressed very clearly in this book. The moment that hit me so hard was not the finding out; it was realizing how deep the effect went.

I was stopped in my tracks the day after her hysterectomy. I went to the hospital. She was slowly getting up as I walked in the room. She looked right at me and said, "Everything that makes me female is gone." I froze. This was not the Denika I know. For those who know her, she is the walking embodiment of femininity. She does not leave the house without full makeup. She puts others before herself: friend, family, and strangers. She runs a perfect house. She is the ultimate nurturer and the best mother I know. How could she even think this?

The good news is, that was but a blip. Breast cancer (and all that happens because of it) would cause any woman to think this. Next to dying, it's what scares all of us. What I hope you get from reading this book is she went through it all. She came out the other end whole: just as strong, resilient, fun, and feminine. If you are looking for a role model, she is one.

Sheila Keats
Friend

* * *

As one who has walked with Denika through her courageous battle, I would be so honored to briefly share my story from the outside looking in.

Denika confided in me how she had found a lump on the side of her breast the summer of 2015. The lump was big, noticeable, and very scary. I feared for my friend and I prayed for her in the days to come.

Denika called me and shared the results of her biopsy and I will never forget the sound in her voice. It was a sound I never heard before coming from my vivacious, positive, full-of-life friend. It was a sound of fear and worry but yet optimism. Before we hung up she reassured me (because that's who she is: reassuring even in her time of hopelessness) that she will fight this fight. And, before we said goodbye, I believed her.

In the following weeks she knew she would soon have to shave her head. For a woman to have to do that is very hard. A woman's hair is her crown and she was about to set it aside.

I went to Denika's home the day we were to begin embracing her new look. To my surprise it wasn't somber or heart-wrenching at all; it was rather the complete opposite. Some of Denika's family members were there laughing, carrying on, and supporting her. It was a very positive day and she was so strong. That day as I drove away from her home I knew Denika Philpott was gonna beat cancer; there was no doubt in my mind.

It's been just over one year since the dreaded diagnosis was brought down upon my friend. A Facebook status can only give us all a mere glimpse into what she endured; we will truly never know just how hard she's fought. Unless you've gone through it, it's hard to know the amount of teardrops or sleepless nights she and her amazing family had suffered through. But what we can all gain through following Denika's journey is this: For those who don't know her well, or for those who do, you can certainly know that she is a fighter. Through her story she will reach other cancer patients and survivors along with their families. She will bring hope when it seems to be lost.

Denika, I am so proud of you. I might not get to tell you enough, but you are a warrior woman. You've truly come out stronger and more beautiful than ever. I'm so very happy you came into my life several years ago and I'll always be rooting for you, girl.

Kayla Loveless
Hair Stylist and Friend

* * *

If you read one book this year to help you become more positive, honest and thankful for life . . . this has to be it! This book is full of inspiration with the attitude of a true warrior. A masterful work full of courage, honesty, and, above all, love. I completed the book through tears and was so moved that I had to read it in segments. This beautiful book is unlike any other personal account of living with breast cancer that I have ever read. This provoking, raw account of her experience offers patients and families practical insights into how they can live their love for life more fully and derive meaning from their journey amidst the heartbreak of a horrible illness.

I stand in awe of Denika's honesty, determination, courage, and the majesty of her love of life. It is an eloquent and honest account of a long ordeal. It transcends pain and loss and becomes an inspiration in a heart-felt, honest, and tender manner. This book by an overcomer has the potential to be an enormous help to those facing cancer or walking with a loved one on a similar journey.

Angela Lily
Life Coach and Motivational Speaker
www.angelalily.com
CBS, Newfoundland Labrador

* * *

Connected! That is the word which might best describe the decision Denika made to share her journey through the perils of the diagnosis of cancer. It has been a real privilege to walk with Denika as editor during the preparation of her book. Our many, many exchanges of emails and draft manuscripts have become my opportunity to have a window into the life of this amazing woman being fashioned by God. Her book, Overcomer, now allows you, the reader, to join her and her many "friends" from Facebook to "connect by heart" with her journey. She openly shares about dreadful moments and dire pain-filled reactions to the treatments. But, she also shares about discoveries made on that journey. "Connected" took on a whole new meaning in one of her lowest points. Overcoming for Denika was possible as she was undergirded by her faith in her Living Lord. Her discoveries and the shared journey of this courageous "lion-like" lady await you as you now hold her book in your hand.

Rev. Peggy I. Kennedy
Two Silver Trumpets Ministries
Speaker & Author
Beamsville, Ontario
www.TwoSilverTrumpets.ca

My friend Vahen and I

Denika and I have known each other since grade school and we have shared many great memories. Now, as I read her book, Overcomer, it is clear that this is going to be a powerful testimony of God's sustaining power. And, it is a memory that will go down in history. I myself have endured some deep emotional and physical pain, but as I read Denika's story, I struggled with trying to relate to the magnitude of her pain. I found myself thinking, "I could not have handled that." God truly does give each person the measure of strength needed for their own unique struggles. Denika's story made me think of the words of Song of Solomon 8:5 "Who is this? Look at her now! She arises out of her desert, clinging to her beloved." (Passion Translation)

Overcomer is a remarkable story of one woman's inner strength and bravery to cling to her Heavenly Father for everything she needs.

As you read this book, you will be challenged and inspired to see that with God all things are possible and to seek for more of God's strength in your own life to overcome. To quote Denika herself, "He is the author of my story and He will be glorified in the end. That alone gave me so much hope that I had no choice but to smile, hold my head high…" The quote of a true warrior.

It is clear that Denika is on God's assignment. She has proven that "No weapon formed against her will prosper." Watch for her quote in this book: "The devil whispers, You can't withstand the storm." The warrior replied, "I am the storm." Denika, You indeed are a warrior and an overcomer!

Vahen King
Licensed minister
Pentecostal Assemblies of Alberta & Northwest Territories
Speaker, Author, Life Coach
Edmonton, AB
www.vahenking.com

* * *

In Loving Memory

My Niece ~ Shakira Rideout
My Aunt ~ Kathy Philpott

I am going to a city,
Where the streets with gold are laid;
Where the tree of life is blooming
And the roses never fade.

Here they bloom but for a season
Soon their beauty is decayed.
I am going to a city,
Where the roses never fade.
In this world we have our troubles,
Satan snares we must evade.
We'll be free from all temptations;
Where the roses never fade.

Loved ones gone to be with Jesus,
In their robes of white arrayed;
Now are waiting for my coming,
Where the roses never fade.

Here they bloom but for a season
Soon their beauty is decayed.
I am going to a city,
Where the roses never fade.

From Where the Roses Never Fade
by Janie West Metzgar ©, 1927-1935

Dedication

I would like to dedicate Overcomer to my Mom, Ella Philpott. Mom was diagnosed with breast cancer in January of 1997. She had a mastectomy but thankfully, no treatments were needed. I learned so much as I watched how Mom handled that very difficult time in her life. I remember asking her, "Mom, why you?" Her reply? "Why not me?" She had zero self-pity and was so strong. Her faith in God carried her and for the past 19 years, she has been cancer-free. Mom, you are my hero.

I would also like to dedicate this book to anyone who has had to hear the words, "You have cancer." That very statement not only changes your life, it changes you as a person. So to all who have had to have chemotherapy, surgeries, and radiation, this book is for you. To those with us and to those who have passed on. You fought the good fight.

> *"I have fought the good fight,*
> *I have finished the race,*
> *I have kept the faith."*
> *2 Timothy 4:7*

"For I know the plans I have for you," declares the LORD, "plans to prosper you and not to harm you, plans to give you hope and a future."

Jeremiah 29:11

Table of Contents

Acknowledgments

For years I have wanted to write a book. I had made an attempt once but I never did finish it. Then I was handed my diagnosis and began the journey from which this book is drawn. From the day I laid pen to paper my husband, Darryl Pike, encouraged me. As he isn't a reader I would read out each chapter to him as it was completed and I'd look to see the tears rolling down his face. Thank you for everything, Darryl: for adding your perspective, for giving me that boost when I was struggling, and for advising me to take a break when I became overwhelmed. You sat by me and grieved as I grieved, cried as I cried, and laughed as I laughed.

Mom and Dad, throughout the writing of this book I would run things by you, only to be met with silence and pain. I now know that this journey has been harder on you than it has been on me. I know you support my book and I know you're proud of me.

To my children, Noah and Abigail: right from very beginning you both knew I could do this. You had faith in me and were very patient when I would sit you down and read each chapter to you. Thank you for your love, support, and genuine interest. You are my little up-lifters, my little cheering squad, and I love you so much.

Michele, what a faithful sister you are to me. I remember the day I read my manuscript to you over the phone. You were encouraging and honest. Throughout my journey and the writing of this book, you were one of my biggest supporters and up-lifters. I so appreciate you and all that you are.

Thank you, Pastor Bruce Newman, for writing the Foreword. You and Rochelle have seen my journey first-hand over the past year. You can attest to how God worked miracles in my life. Your faithful, consistent care has been a major component of how He has answered prayer.

Peggy Kennedy, how you came to be my editor was nothing short of a miracle. When I realized this book was actually going to be published, I contacted Vahen King as she had published her book with you as her editor shortly before. When she suggested I contact Peggy Kennedy to edit my book, I mulled it over, prayed about it, and decided that you were the one!

After connecting with you and beginning the initial steps in the editing process, I knew this relationship was going to be another one that would influence me. As we journeyed through this process, you not only edited my book, but me as well. Your constant reminders of grace and your understanding of where I was coming from, especially during my moments of bitterness and anger, helped me grow as a person. I thank you from the bottom of my heart for being my guide.

Thank you, Vahen and Vaughan King, for helping me throughout the process of publishing. Your openness and wisdom helped make this so much easier.

Thank you, Nancy Wheeler and Wanda Stead, for our photoshoots. Your patience and understanding were exactly what I needed. Also, thank you Darryl and Michele for taking the photos I used for the front cover and the back of my book.

Tammy Tetford, thank you for inspiring me to title this book Overcomer. That title has become part of my encouragement as I've been telling my story. Thank you to my proofreaders: Jasmine Kean and Tammy Tetford.

Thank you in advance to my readers. I pray this book touches your heart. For all of you who encouraged me to write this book and constantly reassured me that I could do it, it is a shared victory. I appreciate you so much.

And abundant thanks to you, God, my Lord and Saviour. You have been my co-author. It is You who gently nudged me to write this book, who encouraged me every day, and led the words that spilled onto the pages that we now hold in our hands. You have made me an *Overcomer*! Lord, bless this book that it may inspire and uplift those who read it.

Foreword

"After a while I looked in the mirror and realized...wow...after all those hurts, scars, and bruises, after all of those trials, I really made it through. I did it. I survived that which was supposed to kill me. So I straightened my crown...and walked away like a boss." (Source Unknown)

Anyone who has ever had the privilege of meeting Denika would say a resounding "Amen" to this quote. Denika is one of the most positive and encouraging people you will ever come across. She is real, raw, and authentic. Even through the considerable trials she has faced from the beginning of her diagnosis to the closing chapter, she has consistently lived the life of an overcomer. Any conversation we have had, meant to encourage her, had me walking away being the one who was encouraged. Through her greatest storm, she was strong and steadfast.

Some of my most poignant memories during this time in Denika's life include seeing her in the church congregation on Sunday with tears streaming down her face, arms raised towards heaven, praising God in the midst of her trial. Often, her son Noah or daughter Abigail had their arms around her to help her remain standing. Her colorful bandana of the day would be streaming down her neck and resting over her painful radiation site. She was the true, physical representation of the scripture we read in Genesis 50:20 concerning the life of Joseph: what the enemy intended for evil in her life, God has turned it for His good and His purposes.

What you are about to delve into is an encouraging account

of the day-to-day battle of a woman of God in the midst of a devastating cancer diagnosis. You're about to read a real life story of struggle and pain. There are no masks in this book. It is an authentic account of her sadness and struggle, but also of her journey with God in the midst of it.

I encourage everyone to read her story. We all face trials in some shape or form throughout our lives. It's not a question of "if," but rather "when." How we handle these circumstances we find ourselves in will determine our character. It is comforting to know that other people have faced struggles and questioned, "Why me?" We can all identify the doubts that often accompany our struggles. Denika's story tells us that we are never alone and that while friends and family are crucial to our overcoming trials, it is the strength, peace, and hope that can only come from the Lord that enables us to make it through.

Bruce Newman
Lead Pastor
Bethesda Pentecostal Church
St. John's, Newfoundland

Introduction

Join my husband and I, my children, my Mom, Dad, and siblings, plus a host of friends on Facebook and others sent by God above, on this journey of *Overcoming*.

From the moment I received my diagnosis of aggressive Stage 3 breast cancer on October 8, 2015, I knew that my life and the lives of those around me were about to change—drastically. I always thought of myself as a strong person but never did I have to be as brave, resilient, and determined. Never did I have to face a fear such as this. Cancer threatened to take me from my family: most people's worst fear.

When I learned from the surgeon what my treatment plan looked like, I had to pull on my armour and fight for my life. Daily I would listen and sing along with my playlist while I cried out to God. I would claim healing and pray for strength and well-being throughout this journey.

As you read *Overcomer*, you will feel the hurts, the disappointments, the fear, the pain, the worry, and many more emotions I experienced. You will also feel the victory, the joy, and the many celebrations I was blessed with along the way.

Sit back, pour a cup of tea, grab some tissues, and walk with me through 2015-2016 as I battle the biggest giant of my life. Watch how God worked everything for His good and made me an *Overcomer*.

Chapter One

An Uncertain Discovery

Pralines and Cream Dream, my favorite Laura Secord ice cream, in a waffle cone of course. That's what I was enjoying when I found it.

It was July 2015 and weather-wise, one of the worst summers I could remember. With the weather really keeping us from doing much else, my 11-year-old daughter Abigail and I decided to spend a few hours at the Avalon Mall in St. John's.

After an hour of browsing through the shops, she wanted to visit the only ice cream shop she knew of that serves her favorite ice cream: Super Kid. She was ordering and getting more excited by the minute about the little chocolate that comes on top of her treat. I was crossing my right arm across my chest while tucking my hand underneath my left armpit as I attempted to hold my ice cream in my left hand.

Then I felt it. Something round and hard in the side of my left breast about the size of a small egg.

"Abigail, come here, feel that."

With eyes wide as saucers she said, "Mommy, that's a lump!"

I looked down at my beautiful little girl and my mind flooded with all the what-if's. With my knees weak and my hands trembling from fear, I took her hand and made my way home.

* * *

Previously, back in 2013, I had found a lump in my left armpit that quickly grew to the size of a small egg. It was very tender and uncomfortable as you can imagine. I approached my family doctor and she sent me for an ultrasound, which then led to a mammogram. Yes, they actually performed a mammogram on a lump in my armpit. Ladies, you who have experienced a mammogram can appreciate how painful and awkward this was.

The results came back saying it was actually breast tissue that had moved up into my armpit. My thoughts? "Great, just what I needed, a third boob."

It was very dense and hard to see through but it looked clear. I wasn't convinced. I've been told for years that I have dense breast tissue so this did not come as a surprise to me. The fact that they weren't 100% sure there was nothing hiding in that mass wasn't good enough for me so I asked for a biopsy. Although my GP didn't see the need, I did. I pushed for the biopsy and finally got it.

The experience of my biopsy is a story in and of itself. A plastic surgeon who will remain anonymous was chosen to do my biopsy. Had I known then what I know now I would have opted for someone with more "internal" experience as you will see.

March 18, 2013, was the day of my procedure. As I lay on the operating table with my left arm over my head, the surgeon asked that I hold my left breast away from the site to be biopsied with my right hand. This may not seem like a big deal to most but perhaps if I paint a picture you'll see why this task wasn't as easy as it sounds. My breasts were an I-cup, (weighing in at a whopping 4 ½ pounds) and the biopsy took 45 minutes.

Needless to say, once I realized she had cut my armpit the full width and I could feel the warmth of blood running down my left side onto my back, I had to talk myself out of not freaking out. All of a sudden I felt this sharp prick.

I asked the surgeon, "Did you just give me a needle?" She said, "Why? What did it feel like?" With measured sarcasm I replied, "Like...you...just...gave...me...a...needle." Very nonchalantly the surgeon answered, "Oh, I must have hit a nerve."

Well, THAT made me feel better! Suddenly nurses were all around me, wiggling my toes, laying icepacks on my neck because apparently I had begun to faint. What a surprise. Then I felt a pain, a full body jolt that I had never felt before. I could have sworn my whole body lifted off the bed.

In a panicked and terrified voice I said, "NOW I can feel everything you're doing!" The surgeon's exact words, "I'd better get out. I'm afraid if I continue you'll lose the use of your arm." Gee, how comforting. My career as Sign Language Interpreter would be over in one flick of the scalpel. In a hurry the doctor extracted two biopsies, sewed me up, and sent a very shaken-up me on my way.

A few weeks later I was back at the hospital to get my results from the biopsies this surgeon had taken. It was a good thing my niece was with me at the time because I had a witness to the strange encounter that took place. When the surgeon came in carrying the clipboard with my biopsy results attached, I asked what the findings were. "Oh, nothing really," she replied. I watched her pen swipe over the page. As I glanced at the report I said, "Wait a minute, what does PASH and Stromal Fibrosis mean?" The response was, "I'll be right back" and the surgeon walked out of the room. My niece and I just looked at each other. "What the heck was THAT!?" Smartphone in hand, we googled those two findings. I read down through the articles explaining what they were. By the time the surgeon came back 20 minutes later, we already knew. Her statement was, "I'm going to refer you to another doctor so they can explain to you what this biopsy means. See the lady at the front desk." That was the only explanation I received and then the surgeon was gone!

As you can imagine I walked out of that hospital with no answers and very frustrated. What my niece and I managed to find out through our own investigation was this: *"Breast fibrosis is also termed more formally as 'hyaline fibrosis of stroma', which simply means a variable increase in dense connective breast tissue. It is a very common finding, occurring in up to 7% of suspicious breast lesions examined by biopsy."*[1]

As well, once we googled PASH, we learned that it was an acronym for Pseudo Angiomatous Stromal Hyperplasia and that it's a rare and benign breast lesion. But again, I wanted to hear it from a doctor. From the research I had done, it seemed both stromal fibrosis and PASH should have been painless. But the reality that the egg- size lump I had was very painful caused concern for me.

Another three weeks went by before I saw the doctor who actually knew what she was talking about. She basically explained exactly what I already knew from Google. I then asked the questions I had for her: "What if the lump in my armpit turns into cancer? What if it gets bigger? What if it pains more?" She was very understanding and explained, "For right now there isn't any higher chance of you getting cancer in your armpit than in your breasts." If any changes occurred, I was to go see her immediately and she would send me for

---

1   Halls, Steven. "Breast Fibrosis." Moose & Doc Breast Cancer, 13 November 2016, https://www.google.ca/webhp?sourceid= chrome-instant&ion=1&espd=2&ie=UTF-8&gws_rd=ssl#q= stromal+fibrosis+definition

more tests.

Was I 100% satisfied with that answer? No, not really; but what was I to do?

It took about six months before the pain in my armpit became worse. So, I returned to see the doctor who explained my biopsies to me and she sent me for an ultrasound. Again, the results were clear. I asked about a repeat biopsy but she didn't see the point knowing that nothing was showing up on the tests. This was my status quo for the next 2 years as my husband and my family (especially my father) constantly worried that they were missing something. But again, what could I do?

Chapter Two

Here We Go Again

In the days and months leading up to July 2015 when I found the lump in my left breast, I had shooting pain in that same area but thought nothing of it. I was used to having pain in that general region due to the lump in my armpit that had been my constant companion for the two years since the biopsy and decision that it was benign. Yes, *maybe* benign, but painful.

The morning after I found the lump, I called my family doctor. She was away until August, so I made an appointment to see her August 11th.

The day of my appointment, my doctor felt the lump and passed it off as a cyst. However, an ultrasound was ordered for September 10, 2015, just to be sure. Because I had had a mammogram in March 2015 and it came back clear there was no need to have another one, or so she thought.

September 10th was on a Thursday. I drove myself to St. Clare's hospital for the ultrasound as my husband was working. As I proceeded to undress "from the waist up" and was positioned on the bed waiting for the cold gel to touch my skin, I started getting butterflies in my stomach. Questions started racing through my mind. I longed for my husband of just 4 years to be there with me, holding my hand. Unfortunately, his job took him 120 kilometers away from our home to a project located in Long Harbour, Newfoundland and Labrador.[1]

Squaring my shoulders, I focused on the doctor who was conducting my ultrasound. After a very thorough search, she said she couldn't see a thing and so she wanted to send me for a mammogram right away. Immediately all I could envision was that cold, unforgiving machine squeezing my breast with the very painful lump. I was filled with dread.

Slowly I made my way down the hall toward the mammography waiting room to wait my turn. The room held about 50 chairs, mostly filled with ladies and their spouses. I couldn't remember another time when I felt so alone and so scared.

With shaking hands, I texted my husband and family members in an attempt to both keep busy and keep them informed. My mind was racing. It felt like my brain was spinning a mile a minute while all the time I was trying not to focus on the "what if's".

To put my situation into context, I was a larger chested woman and all my life had been used to wearing only V-neck shirts, NEVER stripes! I had to purchase my undergarments at a specialty lingerie boutique in order to get the proper fit. Even a bathing suit had to be bought there. How much change was about to swallow up my life? Was I about to lose my life as I had known it for the past 30 years?! As I sat mulling this over, I prayed, "God please, give me strength." No other words would come.

Soon I was standing in front of that dreaded machine holding

---

1   An amendment to the Constitution officially changed the name of Newfoundland to Newfoundland and Labrador on December 6, 2001 The official abbreviations are: Newfoundland Nfld. Newfoundland and Labrador N.L. I will use the common name of "Newfoundland" throughout the remainder of the book as Islanders tend to do. https://www.collectionscanada.gc.ca/obj/040006/f2/040006-02-e.pdf

on to the handlebars for dear life. As the two cold plates squeezed my left breast, one on top and one on bottom, the pain started shooting up my neck and down my left arm. The empathetic technician said, "Honey, let me get you a chair. You look like you're going to pass out." I closed my eyes and replied, "No, please just get it done and over with."

Once the two images were done, the technician looked at me with eyes full of pity and regret, "My darling, I'm so sorry; I didn't get a clear picture and we have to do it again."

When the procedure was finally over and I was walking to my car, I thought to myself, "What in the world is causing me so much pain?" I had had mammograms done before and had never felt this when they were finished. I sat in my car in the parking lot of St. Clare's hospital and could not believe the agony radiating up my neck and down into the muscles of my left arm. Although I have a high tolerance for pain, it was enough to cause tears. As they slowly trickled down my face, I pulled out of the parking lot and headed for home.

Chapter Three

A Ticking Time Bomb

I was awake the whole night in terrible agony. I paced the floor, took an anti-inflammatory pill, and I even tried a technique I learned years ago when I had a pinched nerve in my C2, C3 vertebrae that affected my left arm. I would dig my fingertips into my bicep area to push on the nerve to alleviate the aching. Mind you, I am a Sign Language Interpreter so the only thing I could think was "How on earth am I supposed to work like this?"

Needless to say, that question became even more poignant the next morning. When I awoke, the lump had grown to the size of my fist! I stood in front of the full-length mirror in my bathroom and could not believe what I was seeing. My left breast was bruised along the left side near my armpit and all along the bottom. Having a career where it is VERY difficult to get someone to cover for you, I knew I had no choice but to go to work. The pain I endured that morning was very evident on my face and in the way I held my arms up for signing. Even the Deaf person I was working with noticed.

As soon as I had a break from work, I went straight to my family doctor. Upon arrival I was told she was gone on a holiday so I had to see someone else. This substitute doctor told me not to worry: "It's probably just inflammation from the procedure." He gave me pain killers and sent me back to work without examining me. I worked all weekend and throughout the next week until I could not take it anymore. The following Thursday I went back to see my family doctor as she was now back in the office.

My eyes filled with tears as I sat on the edge of my chair explaining the terrible pain and pure agony I had experienced over the past week. She listened but I could tell she wasn't convinced. Finally, she asked to examine me. It was when I removed "everything from the waist up" she could physically SEE what kind of a state I was in. Please excuse the language, these are not my words. Her exact words were *"OH MY JESUS, DENIKA!"* She wouldn't even touch me because it looked so painful (and it was!). Finally, someone was listening and hopefully could help me.

She suspected it was a cyst inside of a cyst and that the mammogram had possibly "broken" it causing it to bleed internally. She suggested I wear a sling on that arm to limit use so the blood could reabsorb. She signed for a medical leave for me from work.

She booked an appointment for me for October 22, 2015, with a surgeon whom she raved about saying, "He will get to the bottom of this. This doctor is a thinker and will figure out what's going on." I pleaded with her to order me a MRI and a biopsy. After much persuading, she agreed and sent off the request.

When you're thrown into a situation where your future hangs in the balance, you drift into a fog which is exactly where I was during this whole ordeal. You'd think CANCER is what I was thinking all this time, but it wasn't. Looking back, I think I was in denial.

Over the next few weeks my left breast got bigger and

bigger to the point that I walked into the speciality lingerie shop, explained my situation, and asked for the biggest nursing bra they had. Thank God these ladies had what I was looking for. Needless to say, my wardrobe had to change. Because of the tumour, nothing fit anymore! I had to buy baggy sweaters and wear the biggest t-shirts in my closet.

I basically took all this in stride. I wasn't trembling in fear because I didn't have a clue what was to come. Denial was my defense mode. This is evident in my words as taken directly from my journal September 4, 2015, *"September 10th I have a u/s on my left breast. Found a lump the size of a small egg. Dr. says she thinks it's a cyst inside of a cyst. Hopefully it's nothing and can be easily remedied."* I read that now and the tears fall. I ache as I recall what was actually in store for me.

When September 17th arrived, I was still waiting for the radiologist to "review" the doctor's request for my MRI. Apparently, they have to approve it. Until then you wait as it continues to grow. I've never felt so helpless in my life.

The pain became so severe that on September 20th I wrote on Facebook: *"Who thought unloading a dishwasher could cause so much agony?! If anyone has any connections with speeding up MRI's, could you please use your pull for me? I have to get to the bottom of this. #painpaingoaway Thank God for my amazing 13-year-old son who is picking up the slack at home."*

"I'm in pure agony, can't even describe it. Best I can do: it is like a giant toothache from my chest all the way down my left arm."

Finally, 13 days after the mammogram that caused bruising, swelling, and extreme pain, a friend who worked in the MRI unit got me in quicker than my appointed time. It's scary that it's who you know in a situation like this that could potentially save your life.

September 25th, 2015 Facebook status: *"Never been in so much pain before as last night and again this morning. New bruising and grossly swollen. Need results from this MRI ASAP. Needless to say I'm happy hubby has the next 4 days off."*

September 28, 2015 Facebook status: *"Update: MRI results are in. I have to go for a biopsy. Lots of scary stuff going on so please say a prayer for me. Thank you SO MUCH to the amazing support. I truly have the best family and friends...and by far the best husband anyone could ask for."*

Finally, on September 30th I received my appointment for the biopsy. It was set for October 14th. Regretfully, I had to wait 2 full weeks with this thing rapidly growing inside me. The helplessness one feels is truly hard to put into words. You feel like a ticking time bomb. The sleepless nights, heightened stress levels, and inability to concentrate were really taking their toll on me.

Throughout the stress, pain, and worry, I found myself talking to God more and more often. My friends were sending me songs and verses that I could hold onto and it was one of the main things that helped get me through this horrible time.

We think we know what we need. We pray and ask God specifically for this or that, but only He knows what we need. I experienced so many little miracles during this time of turmoil. People I really didn't expect would come around bringing food, flowers, cards or just a chat.

How God works through people during a time like this is truly amazing. Jeremiah 29:11 has been the verse I have stood on for many years. *"For I know the plans I have for you,"* *declares the Lord, "plans to prosper you and not to harm you, plans to give you hope and a future."* Once again I hung onto this verse daily as a reminder that I have Him with me in all of this. He is the author of my story and He will be glorified in the end. That alone gave me so much hope that I had no choice but to smile, hold my head high, and work to get to the bottom of this.

* * *

The doorbell rang on October 2nd. My neighbour, who at the time had 3 very young children, was standing there with a huge bouquet of flowers in her hands. That one gesture meant so much at such a scary time that I began to weep and fell into her arms. As we got to talking, she sensed my urgency in needing this biopsy done. She mentioned someone she knew in Corner Brook who performs ultrasound biopsies. She said she would call him and see if he can help. Within 24 hours, my biopsy appointment that wasn't supposed to happen until October 14th, got moved to October 5th. Albeit it was almost 700 kilometers from where we live but we didn't care. We needed answers! I want to extend my sincere thanks to her for doing as God had prompted her to do.

The way this all happened was one of those little miracles I was telling you about. My little message on Facebook one night stated: *"I wish my parents and siblings could be around me right now."* That message touched my neighbour. She jumped in her truck, went to the store, bought me flowers, and came to my house. From that conversation, this biopsy happened 9 days earlier than it was supposed to. I often wonder if those 9 days made a difference in my treatment success. God does work in mysterious ways.

We drove to Pasadena (half hour from Corner Brook) on Sunday and stayed with our friends for the night. Then Monday morning hubby and I were pleased as punch to realize that my Mom and Dad who had been driving home from Nova Scotia had just got off the ferry and were heading to Corner Brook as well! (Another one of many of the little miracles we were blessed with along the way.) We met them for breakfast before my procedure along with my cousin who was working in Corner Brook at that time.

In Corner Brook. Breakfast with Dad and Mom.

Once my husband and I arrived at the hospital and I got to meet my neighbour's friend, I felt totally at ease. His professional, calm demeanour had me thanking God for putting me there with him. In a few minutes, the biopsy was done, ice was applied to the site, and we were on our way back home.

The next few days were a mixture of fear, gratefulness, and tears. I received so much love and support from family and friends in the way of texts, posts on Facebook, and visits. This is what carried me through.

Chapter Four

The Moment Everything Changed

On October 7, 2015, while sitting in my library waiting for my 13-year-old son and 11-year-old daughter to get home from school, my doctor's Administrative Assistant called me. Her message was brief and to the point: "Denika, the doctor wants to see you tomorrow at 12:30. She wants you to bring your husband."

I said, "Ok," and hung up the phone. Those words hit me like a sledgehammer. I gripped my phone and fell completely apart like I had never fallen apart before. The sounds that escaped from me were like those of a terrified, screaming animal—caged, fighting its prey. I felt the danger I was in, almost as a premonition of what I was facing.

This is the moment my life changed forever.

Sobs and wails continued to pour out of me. The tears were like rivers that I thought would never end. I called my husband immediately to relay what she had said. We knew it wasn't going to be good news. Suddenly I looked at the clock. My son would be home in minutes so I had no choice but to dry my tears and try to look "normal."

The next day by 12:30 p.m. Darryl and I arrived to the doctor's office, took our seats, and waited. I had all my family on my cell phone on a text group chat so that I could relay to them as quickly as possible what my diagnosis was. When my family doctor came in she was visibly shaking, thus confirming what I already knew. She took both my hands in hers and with tears in her eyes she said, "Denika, you have breast cancer."

October 9, 2015 Facebook status: *"For those of you who have stood by me and supported me for the past month, I received my report from my biopsy yesterday, I have breast cancer. Needless to say, it has been a tough month.*

The amount of love and compassion that has been poured out to my family and me is appreciated more than you will ever know, but our battle is only just beginning; I need you now more than ever.

A couple of people have asked me why I post something so personal here, on Facebook, for all to see. Well, I need you. I need support, I need help and I need love. Yes I am THAT needy, lol!!

If you know me at all, you KNOW I will get through this but it will be in part because of my family and friends.

If you're a praying person, please pray, for my husband, my children, my Mom and Dad (both sets), for my siblings, my nieces and nephew and for me."

* * *

I wish I could say everyone helped me and supported me through this past year. Unfortunately, as others who have gone through illness, divorce, financial struggles, or identity crisis will tell you, some who you thought would stand by you were the very ones who did not. Thankfully, the throngs of positive, praying, and supportive people far outweighed the other. This abundant support along with everything my God has done for me is what lifted me over those tumultuous seas that threatened to pull me under.

Once this post went up, the messages, songs, and gifts I received bowled me over! The kindness and sincerity of people became armour for my fight. I felt like each gift and each message became the shield, the sword, and the helmet; if cancer wanted to fight, I was ready! So right here now I say thank you to every single person who reached out to me in a positive way.

* * *

On October 9th a good friend sent me the link to a song by Darlene Zschech titled "In Jesus Name,"[1] the live version. That was the first of a playlist I created from inspirational, uplifting songs people sent me. I leaned heavily on the words to these songs daily. (I still do.) I clicked on the link and turned it up, LOUD. As she sang, I cried, sobbed, and paced the floor of my bedroom. I prayed to God and rebuked the devil, telling him he wasn't going to win this fight. I armed myself with the lyrics from this song and others. Another two of my friends suggested I listen to "No Longer a Slave"[2] by Jonathan David & Melissa Helser. The more I listened to this song, the more it spoke to me. I would sing these every morning. As this journey

1   Darlene Zschech. "In Jesus' Name from Darlene Zschech's #RevealingJesus Project." Online video clip. *Youtube.* 26 March 2013. Web. 11 October 2016.

2   Bethel Music. "Music Moment: No Longer Slaves - Jonathan & Melissa Helser." Online video clip. *Youtube.* 10 October 2016. Web. 11 October 2016.

took me deeper into my cancer treatments, I would sing them waiting to fall asleep in the OR and lying on the bed waiting for radiation treatments.

This is a list of songs people sent me during the time of my treatments that became my playlist: "Oceans Deep,"[3] "I Will Look Up"[4] by Elevation Worship, "I Will Rest"[5] by North Point, "Just Be Held"[6] by Casting Crowns, "He Won't Leave You There"[7] by Jason Crabb, "Healing is Here"[8] by Deluge, "Steady Heart"[9] by Steffany Gretzinger, "Overcomer"[10] by Mandisa, "Songs in the Night"[11] by Matt Redman, "He Knows

3 David309211. "Oceans (Where Feet May Fail) - Hillsong United (Zion)." Online video clip. *Youtube.* 23 February 2013. Web. 11 October 2016.

4 Elevation Worship. "I Will Look Up" – LIVE." Online video clip. *Youtube.* 13 January 2014. Web. 11 October 2016.

5 Northpointmusic. "North Point InsideOut: Hear - I Will Rest (Adam Kersh)." Online video clip. *Youtube.* 1 July 2015. Web. 11 October 2016.

6 CastingCrownsVEVO. "Casting Crowns - Just Be Held (Official Lyric Video)." Online video clip. *Youtube.* 27 January 2014. Web. 11 October 2016.

7 Jason Crabb. "Jason Crabb LIVE - "He Won't Leave You There." Online video clip. *Youtube.* 16 November 2015. Web. 11 October 2016.

8 Johnny Powell. "Deluge - Healing Is Here (Live)." Online video clip. *Youtube.* 17 April 2012. Web. 11 October 2016.

9 Bethel Music. "Steady Heart" Steffany Gretzinger- Live acoustic version."Online video clip. *Youtube.* 11 October 2014. Web. 11 October 2016.

10 MandisaVEVO. "Mandisa – Overcomer." Online video clip. *Youtube.* 12 September 2013. Web. 11 October 2016.

11 Wilbert Hartman. "Songs In The Night - Matt Redman (Unbroken Praise)." Online video clip. *Youtube.* 17 June 2015. Web. 11 October 2016.

What He's Doing"[12] by Jason Crabb, "Fight Song"[13] by Rachel Platten, "Rooftops"[14] by Jesus Culture, "You Make Me Brave"[15] by Amanda Cook, "It Is Well"[16] by Kristene Dimarco, "We Dance"[17] by Steffany Gretzinger, "I Didn't Fall in Love With Your Hair"[18] by Brett Kisswel, and "Trust in You"[19] by Lauren Daigle.

---

12 Jason Crabb. "Jason Crabb LIVE - "He Knows What He's Doing." Online video clip. *Youtube.* 19 August 2015. Web. 11 October 2016.

13 MusicWithMeaning. "Fight Song - Rachel Platten | Lyrics." Online video clip. *Youtube.* 21 March 2015. Web. 11 October 2016.

14 JesusCultureVEVO. "Jesus Culture – Rooftops." Online video clip. *Youtube.* 23 November 2010. Web. 11 October 2016.

15 Bethel Music. "You Make Me Brave - Amanda Cook & Bethel Music (Official Live Music Video)." Online video clip. *Youtube.* Youtube, 5 April 2014. Web. 11 October 2016

16 Bethel Music. "It Is Well - Kristene DiMarco & Bethel Music - You Make Me Brave." Online video clip. *Youtube.* 27 April 2014. Web. 11 October 2016.

17 Bethel Music. "We Dance (Official Lyric Video) - Steffany Frizzell Gretzinger & Bethel Music - You Make Me Brave." Online video clip. *Youtube.* 24 April 2014. Web. 11 October 2016.

18 BrettKissel. "Brett Kissel (ft. Carolyn Dawn Johnson) - I Didn't Fall In Love With Your Hair - Official Video." Online video clip. *Youtube.* 22 September 2016. Web. 11 October 2016.

19 LaurenDaigleVEVO. "Lauren Daigle - Trust In You." Online video clip. *Youtube.* 15 August 2015. Web. 11 October 2016.

Chapter Five

Unprepared for the
Long Road Ahead

Let me take you back to 2014. My husband, to whom I have been married for 5 years on July 21st, 2016, asked me what he could do for me. Wow! Loaded question! Both my kids said simultaneously, "Mom has always wanted a library." I said, "Now guys, I don't think that's what he means." Always up for a challenge he says, "Hmmm, wait now; let me think."

Over the next few weeks we talked about what I envisioned: the size, how many bookshelves, and what kind of wood I wanted on the walls and ceiling. Within a week he had it started. It became a true labour of love. Almost to the day of the last nail being driven and my library being complete, I received my diagnosis. Little did we know that it would become my recovery room from a very aggressive form of breast cancer. Another one of our miracles.

Another example of the little miracles we experienced that actually came into place before we really knew how much we'd need them happened on October 10th. Here is my Facebook post for that day: *"Today I am thankful for family, near and*

My Library. Hubby's labour of love for me.

far. For my sister Angela who has a faith that led her to follow God's gentle whisper to order a book a full month ago, even though she had no idea who for (she already owns it). Two days ago it arrived in the mail, two days ago I received my diagnosis. WOW! #powerful."

The things you learn along a journey such as this are astounding. For example, I have been told that in women with dense breast tissue, such as myself, mammograms perhaps only detect 25% of tumours. I have been told that mammograms are very important. Having one saved my mother's life in 1997. However, I feel strongly that more should be done for early detection. On September 10th, I had an ultrasound and a mammogram. Both were clear; no cancer showed although there was a tumour the size of a small egg. Very scary. Had I not pushed for a MRI and biopsy, what would have become of me?

Facebook post October 14th: *"So just to let people know....an ultrasound AND mammogram did NOT detect my breast cancer. Because my breasts are very dense, fibrous as the doctor called it, the only way breast cancer was detected with me was MRI. Ultrasound and mammogram on Sept 10 show NO CANCER, MRI on Sept 23 showed cancer.*

Please don't put all your faith in mammograms if you have dense breast tissue. It is the MRI that saved my life. It could be exactly what you would want to insist on, too."

My surgeon's appointment scheduled for October 22nd loomed. I couldn't wait for it to come, yet I felt frozen with fear and dread. I knew the MRI that I had on September 23rd said I had breast cancer but the extent of treatment was unknown at this point. I thought maybe a mastectomy of the left breast and radiation. Here is what I posted a few days before that appointment:

"So it's been a tough few days. I said I would journey this with my Facebook friends who care, and I will. So here goes: These past 2 days have been turmoil. I have wanted to sob, heartbreakingly cry, move back in with my Mom and Dad, and hide in a corner and not come out. But I didn't. I didn't want to interrupt anyone's life and say please, I need a hug....no wait, a 30 second hug, I need to cry. My surgeon's appt is this Thursday and I don't know what he's going to say. I don't know what the next few months hold for me and I'm scared. Simple as that."

The wait from that day until the actual appointment felt like a year. I kept busy, watched uplifting, inspirational videos, and listened to my playlist over and over and over. The dismal results of that critical appointment were summarized in detail on my Facebook post:

My Facebook post: *"Ok. So, for all of you following me on this journey, you'll need to sit down. The cancer is aggressive.*

I had blood work today, then the surgeon is going to fast track ordering a CT scan, bone scan and a MRI biopsy of the right breast. Once those test results are back, I will meet with an oncologist, then I will start chemo in 3-4 weeks for around 6 months to attack this thing head on and try to shrink whatever cancer is growing in my body. After that I meet with the surgeon again to book the surgery for mastectomy. Then radiation. Please, please keep my family and I in your prayers."

In that pivotal appointment I've just summarized for you my surgeon very gently said I needed 5-6 months of chemotherapy before he could perform surgery. I was stunned and my mouth fell open. Of course I asked, "Why?" His reply was so alarming: "Well, because, it's a mess in there. The tumour is so big that if we did the surgery now, we would never get it all. We need the chemo to frighten it into a corner, scare it into a little ball, and then we can perform the mastectomy."

I did NOT expect that. As he explained that I would then need a mastectomy and radiation, I realized how serious this was. I felt the world standing completely still. Once he left the room, I started pacing while muttering about having to eat healthier to prepare myself for the arduous road of chemotherapy.

My husband kept repeating his pet name for me, "Hon, hon!" but I was frantic—totally beside myself, until he grabbed me by my shoulders and pulled me into a hug as the tears ran down his face. I felt the heart-wrenching sobs rising up through my chest and spilling from me. We were both in shock and felt so unprepared for what was coming.

Chapter Six

Just One More Time

People may think that words are just that: mere words. But boy do they ever mean a lot when you're in a time of need. The day I posted my diagnosis, one of my friends sent me this quote: *"I've battled my whole life to become the strong woman I am today. If you think you can take me down after all that I've been through, give it your best shot. You will not succeed."* Well, that quote marched its way into my reserve. I sat a little straighter after that, knowing that I will fight this thing head on with the determination of a lion.

> **"The devil whispers "You can't withstand the storm."**
> **The warrior replied "I am the storm."** *(source unknown)*

The next day, October 23rd, Darryl and I went to my parents for the weekend. Thank God for my Mom and Dad. Hearing the diagnosis of breast cancer was hard for my husband and I; but, I simply can't imagine how it must have been for my parents. I am the youngest of four children. As I walked into my parent's house, I fell into my Mom's arms. The sobs that escaped me felt and sounded like I was 4 years old again. I just needed my Mommy to tell me everything was going to be ok.

The next evening as the four of us, Darryl, Mom, Dad, and I were sitting around the kitchen table (our typical gathering place back at home) I felt a sharp jab. It was almost like something hit my breast. Then I could feel that same sharp pain radiating up into my armpit. I could feel something in my left breast changing. I ran to Mom's bathroom and unbuttoned my pajama shirt. When I did, my hand flew to my mouth—my eyes wide as saucers. My breast had changed shape! I couldn't believe it. I yelled out to Darryl to come see. In order to believe it, he had to see it.

Tumor changed, causing intense pain.

Throughout the next month until I began chemotherapy, the same changes kept happening. I would experience stabbing pains or a hot, flooding sensation in my breast. When I would look, it would be bigger or a different shape. I would later learn that this was indicative of the type of breast cancer I was diagnosed with.

*   *   *

Since my family doctor had taken me off work, I had to figure out a way to pay my bills. I knew since I wasn't working I could apply for Sickness Benefits through Employment Insurance. So, on October 22nd I did just that. Sometime during the next week I had a phone call.

Let me help you picture mentally where I was at this time. I was a 41-year-old Mom of two, with an aggressive breast cancer diagnosis. Only days before I had been told what my year would look like: chemotherapy, mastectomy, and radiation. I was so emotionally upset and stressed that I felt like I was spinning.

This phone call from an individual from Employment Insurance left me in tears and visibly shaking. At the beginning of our conversation the questions didn't seem too out to lunch. However, when he started pushing me for the "date I would be going back to work," I became very frustrated. I kept telling him, "I DON'T KNOW!" He did not accept that answer apparently and continued to badger me. Finally, in tears, I said, "Listen, I'm a 41-year-old Mom of two precious children. I have just been diagnosed with a very aggressive form of cancer. I don't know if I'll even be alive next year, much less be working." His reply? "You sound very stressed, so I will let you go."

He turned me down.

I received the letter in the mail a few days later saying they had turned me down for sick benefits. I sat and cried so hard. I couldn't believe someone in his position would be so heartless.

It gets worse.

At this point, I had not worked in a month and my bills were piling up. I called the EI office to see what could be done and was told I had to wait 30 days for an appeal; no if's, and's, or but's. So, my husband suggested I contact someone in a position of authority. Of all the people in authority, we thought this individual would be the most understanding given her medical history. We were confident she would be able to do something. Again, I was shot down. Apparently after someone ticks "no" in a little box on a form, even a letter from God can't overturn that decision.

Considering the tremendous stress I was under at this time, I did NOT need more. I had no choice but to let it go. However, with my husband's gentle nudging, I decided to try one more time. I called the EI office. A friendly female voice answered the phone. I began telling this lady what had happened. As I talked, I paced my house from one end to the other; I ended my story sobbing. She was appalled. She said, "But it says here on your file that you're still working." That statement hit me like a ton of bricks, "WHAT!?" "Yes, that's what it says here. ARE you still working, Ms. Philpott?" In a VERY determined and convincing tone I responded with "NO, and if you saw me you wouldn't have to wonder why!"

This empathetic, understanding lady couldn't believe what had happened to me. With a touch of a button, she overturned that decision and said I should have some money by the following day. She apologized profusely for what I had been through and wished me all the best.

All of that happened because one little box was inaccurately marked on a computer file indicating that I was still working when clearly I wasn't. I had undergone undue stress and frustration. Was it a mistake, a careless error, or was it someone maliciously altering my claim? I tried in earnest to trace how it had happened. However, it was to no avail. I did my best to make sure that no one else would have to deal with such an unjust and unnecessary complication.

Regardless of the source, I knew I had just experienced a divine intervention from the Lord. How else could I explain getting just the right person to answer my call when I tried just one more time. This was critical not only as wonderful encouragement but also essential for my journey going forward.

Chapter Seven

Broken, Bald, and Blessed

We all love our hair. As I was researching chemotherapy, I learned that I would end up losing most or all of it. This was a real struggle for me. Not to sound vain, but I loved my hair. I enjoyed how I could style it a number of ways. I enjoyed how even strangers would walk up to me and tell me how much they loved it. And yet, here I was having to face shaving my head. Every time I thought about it, a knot would form in the pit of my stomach.

One day I received a text from my niece who then posted it to my Facebook page: *"Aunt Denika, I thought of you as soon as I heard this song. You can get through this Aunt D. You have such a strong support system behind you and no matter what your Beena (a nickname I've had for her since she was a baby) will always love you. Like this song says "I didn't fall in love with your hair."* The song was "I Didn't Fall in Love with Your Hair"[1] by Brett Kissel. Again, I sat on the couch and cried so hard I was sure my heart was breaking.

Even though I knew this was MY journey, I felt terrible for

---

1 BrettKissel. "Brett Kissel (ft. Carolyn Dawn Johnson) - I Didn't Fall In Love With Your Hair - Official Video." Online video clip *Youtube*, 22 September 2016. Web. 11 October 2016.

my husband. We had only been married a little over 4 years
and here he was having to deal with his wife having cancer. I
felt that I had cheated him out of a "normal" life with someone
else—someone healthy. I actually contemplated leaving him
so he could go find someone who was not "broken." I was
going to lose my hair. I was going to have to endure whatever
side effects chemotherapy threw at me. I was going to lose my
breasts. (I had decided to have both removed.) Then I would
go through the daily trek to the Cancer Clinic for radiation for
5 weeks. It just seemed so unfair that he be stuck with this. I
said to him a few times, "I'd like to move away to a secluded
cabin by myself for a year, get all this done, and then come
back in order to spare everyone the pain." Needless to say,
he did NOT agree. Darryl has been my rock. I do not know
what I would have done without the constant support and care
from him and my Mom. I would not have been able to wade
through the months ahead.

   Another source of strength and love for me was my friend
Sheila. She and I have an interesting history—one which
brought me one of the best friends I could ever hope to have.
The amount of support this woman gave to me is unmatched.
Her creative care for me included meals, warm fuzzy sweaters,
countless books, or a time to just chat about anything *other
than the cancer.*

   As a side note, you will never hear me call it MY cancer.
It never was mine. It was a very unwelcome presence in my
body; and, I was not so politely asking it to leave ASAP without
taking any prisoners. I called it "the tumour" or "the cancer."
It's lucky I kept its name that nice!

   Over the few weeks leading up to my initial chemotherapy
treatment I had repeated procedures: a MRI biopsy on my right
breast (to check for any cancer in that one), a CT scan, a bone

scan, and a meeting with my oncologist to see what our plans were. The MRI biopsy, which isn't a frequent procedure (thank God), was a little more intense than I had hoped. Because this procedure was on my right breast, I had to lie face down on the table with my left breast (the one with the tumour) squashed against my body. This position caused excruciating pain. The right breast was dangling and gently sandwiched between two plates.

I described the ordeal on my Facebook post: *"So in being authentic and raw, here we go. My biopsy went a little unexpected. The freezing wouldn't take at first (felt the first cut, OWWWW), then MORE freezing. Then the first biopsy apparatus went into my right breast. They rolled me into the MRI machine; meanwhile, I resist the urge to both vomit and pass out. They roll me out only to learn that the biopsy thingy fell out!!! Ugh! Try #2!!!*

New cut, bigger, deeper biopsy thing in, rolling into the machine...again resisting the powerful urge to vomit or pass out by reciting "The Lord is my Shepherd" and visualizing myself in my library, in my recliner wrapped in Mom's quilt.

When it was all said and done, 6 biopsies later, I come home only to find the bleeding has continued and the pain is overwhelming.

So between getting up to get ice, letting the dog in and out, cleaning the wound, I had a rough day.

Yuck.

Hello Atasol 30 (just for tonight.)"

* * *

The October 29th Facebook post centred on the extreme blessing of the creative outpouring of love and support: *"How does one truly express thanks?! From flowers, cards, homemade soup and bread, hugs, freezer full, invitations out—all of this is appreciated more than people realize. Well, today my HUSBAND was gifted. Darryl Pike, this amazing man of honour, courage, and love, works in Long Harbour with a fabulous group of people. I know this because he comes homes with stories of them daily.*

Well today was especially uplifting. In tears he sends me a text.

..."You know the fundraiser the crowd were putting off at work for so-and-so's son's hockey tournament; it was actually for us!"

His colleagues had organized a 50/50 draw, collected a very respectable amount of cash, split it between Darryl and another gentleman whose name was pulled out of a hat who then walked over and handed it to Darryl saying, "Here, for you and Denika for all you're going through."

The goodness of people, the utter selflessness that both Darryl and I have experienced, and the Hand of God in all of this is humbling and praise worthy.

Thank you."

Chapter Eight

Surprise!

Most of my family live here in Newfoundland except for one sister, Michele Fraser. She lives in Strathmore, Alberta. Michele and I are seven years apart and have been close off and on throughout our lives. Michele has known her share of heartache. Her beautiful daughter, Shakira Rideout, passed away at the tender age of 23 years. Michele knows the agony of the ongoing tests, the trips back and forth to the hospital, waiting for results, and getting bad news. Needless to say, she could relate. As time went on, she would make sure to facetime every single day to see how I was. During that facetime "visit" she would make sure my spirits were up. And if they weren't, she would cry with me as I cried.

On October 31st as I was picking my son up from his friend's house, I dropped into my other sister's (Angela's) house for tea. As I was chatting with her, out pops my sister Michele AND my Mom and Dad!!! She had flown in from Strathmore, Alberta and Mom and Dad had driven in the five hours from central Newfoundland to welcome her home and to celebrate with all our family. My brother and his wife who live just down the street from my sister were there too. After I had recovered from nearly passing out from excitement, we had two weeks of great fun. You KNOW you're having fun and laughing a lot when your oldest sister pees herself, not once but twice in her two-week holiday (sorry Michele, I HAD to.)

My sister Michele and I

* * *

November 3rd, I received the results of the left breast ultrasound biopsy I had done in Corner Brook. I now knew the cancer was HER2 positive and ER+. This news brought me into an extensive researching of the specific type of cancer and the typical characteristics.

"HER2 positive breast cancer is a breast cancer that tests positive for a protein called human epidermal growth factor receptor 2 (HER2), which promotes the growth of cancer cells.

In about 1 of every 5 breast cancers, the cancer cells have a gene mutation that makes an excess of the HER2 protein. HER2-positive breast cancers tend to be more aggressive than other types of breast cancer. They're less likely to be sensitive to hormone therapy, though many people with HER2-positive breast cancer can still benefit from hormone therapy."[1]

"Breast cancers are tested to see if they are sensitive to hormones. Approximately 75% of breast cancers have hormone receptors. Cancers that have hormone receptors respond to the female hormones, estrogen and progesterone. When stimulated with these hormones the tumour cells grow and divide. Estrogen receptors are the most common receptors and predict whether the tumour will respond to anti-estrogen therapy."[2]

"The goal of hormone therapy in premenopausal women with breast cancer is to either stop the production of estrogen or block the effect of the estrogen on the breast cancer cells."[3]

I was learning more—much more than I had ever desired to know about the cancer. Everything I read only confirmed that the cancer I had been diagnosed with was treatable. But, I was also very, very sure that I was more than eager for the treatments to start; and, the sooner the better.

* * *

On November 10th I had my first appointment with my oncologist. She would now tell me the results of the tests I had done to see if the cancer had spread anywhere else. As Darryl, Michele, and I waited, we were all very nervous. I

---

1 Moynihan, Timothy J. M.D. "HER2-positive breast cancer: What is it?." Mayo Clinic, 1998-2016 Mayo Foundation for Medical Education and Research, 25 March 2015, http://www.mayoclinic.org/breast-cancer/expert-answers/faq-20058066

2 Ivo Olivotto, M.D, Karen Gelmon M.D, David McCready M.D, and Urve Kuusk M.D, The Intelligent Patient Guide to Breast Cancer (Canada: Library and Archives Canada Cataloguing in Publication, 2014), 82.

3 Ivo Olivotto, M.D, The Intelligent Patient Guide to Breast Cancer, 161

felt almost like an out-of- body feeling. It's surreal when you know your life is about to change, one way or another. And it all depends on a few simple words. This was my post on Facebook immediately after I received the news: *"The cancer hasn't spread anywhere!!!! It's only in my left breast. Praise the Lord!!!!! I may not make much sense because I'm still reeling from this awesome news! Look out, breast cancer!!!! Chemo starts Nov 19 for 6 treatments, then surgery, then radiation.... and I'M GOOD!!! Bring it on!"*

During this whole time, the support I was receiving through Facebook, texts, visits and emails was truly uplifting. Because of the prayer that was being sent up for me, I just knew in my heart that this verse was going to be played out in the next few months:

> *"And we know that for those who love God all things work together for good, for those who are called according to His purpose."* Romans 8:28

At the time of my diagnosis, my son Noah was 13 and my daughter Abigail was 11 years old. As you can appreciate, this journey was tough on them as well. Yes, children ARE very resilient, very positive, and somewhat understanding of the situation. (Do any of us, either as a child or as an adult, truly understand?) But, I'm their Mom and my goal from the beginning was to be honest with them about what to expect but at the same time to not let them see me at my worst. However, pain and sickness does not care who is around; it shows its ugly face whenever it pleases. There were times my children saw me in a great deal of pain, or hunched over making my way to the bathroom.

Every evening after the appointments with my oncologist

when she had to feel around my breast for the tumour for measuring purposes, I would always end up in a great deal of pain. For anyone who has ever experienced nerve pain, you can relate. The lymph nodes were so inflamed that they would press against the nerves causing this awful agony that was impossible to alleviate.

It was after the appointment on November 10th that I was experiencing such agony. All I could do was pace the floors while my sister Michele heated up my lavender heating bag to wrap around the site. Hours later, once the pain had subsided a little, Abigail came to me. "Mommy, I need you to come with me, but cover your eyes and no peeking!" She led me into their rec room where she had spent the last hour. "Ok, you can look now!" As I uncovered my eyes, there in front of me was a painting she had done for me.

Abigail's heartfelt painting

Tears flooded my cheeks as I took in the thoughtfulness and empathy of my little girl. The painting was of her and me—me with a bald head. We had pink ribbons tied to our dresses and we were holding hands. Painted above this sweet picture was "With me by your side you will be ok." In the long weeks and months ahead, as I was lying in my recliner in my library, I could turn my head to the right and there was my painting. It was hung proudly on the wall as a reminder of what I had to fight for.

During the month of November, the pain was constant. I wasn't sleeping very much at all, only 2-3 hours a night. During the day I would try to fit in a nap but that wasn't always possible. You know it's bad when you pray for chemotherapy to start, so if it's successful, you get some type of immediate relief from that pain.

Two days before my first chemotherapy session, my husband got the news that he was laid off. I had not worked since September and at this point I had no income. His layoff was bittersweet in that he would be able to attend my treatments with me but his income would be reduced to Employment Insurance. And, Christmas was coming. Now, in between my prayers for God to give me strength, courage, and healing, I had to add the prayer, "Please help Darryl find another job." As always, He knew what we needed a lot more than we did.

Chapter Nine

In Agony but Not Alone

On November 19th, my first day of chemotherapy, I awoke at 2 a.m. (Little did I know that this would be my routine on chemo days.) At this point, the tumour was measuring 14 x 15 centimeters. Wow!

The first of anything is usually scary and chemotherapy is no different. Doctors and friends who have been through it can try to prepare you. However, we're all different and we all react differently to different things.

One of the chemotherapies can cause an allergic reaction and make you feel as if you're having a panic attack so the nurses had to watch me for that. I ended up not having a reaction like that. I did, however, have excessive heartburn due to the anti-nausea medication. This was so extensive that I had to lift my chin up to try and stop the burning from bubbling up any further. The oncologist on duty prescribed a medication for me and quickly found me some Gaviscon tablets which were very well received.

"The advantage of chemotherapy and other drug therapies such as hormones is that the drugs travel through the blood stream, reaching cancer cells that may be in distant organs. Drug therapies are therefore called systemic treatments because

they attack the cancer through the blood system."[1]

For me, the worst chemotherapy (which I called "the devil") was Taxotere. Because its side effects can be so severe, the oncologist prescribes Dexamethasone (a steroid) to help prevent nausea, fluid retention, and allergic reactions. I had to take this twice the day before chemotherapy, the day of, and the day after. (Later they would increase me to 5 days instead of 3 due to the onslaught of side effects I experienced.) The important thing I had to remember while being on chemotherapy was to not be around anyone who was sick. This is harder than it seems, especially when you're a blended family and children are going back and forth between your home and the other parents' home. If my temperature went to 38 Celsius, we had to go to emergency right away to rule out any infections. This was stressed to us over and over. *"Your white blood cells may decrease 7 days after your treatment. They usually return to normal 15 to 21 days after your last treatment. White blood cells protect your body by fighting bacteria (germs) that cause infection. When they are low, you are at a greater risk of having an infection."*[2]

For me, the battle with the nausea, bone pain, and maintaining a temperature lower than 38 Celsius was knowing what medication I could take and when to take it. I wasn't allowed to take anything that would mask a fever yet it had to reduce pain. As well, I was having some serious stomach issues. My diet was being continually restricted. I was living on bread and tea. Anything else would have me bent over with vicious stomach cramps all evening. Needless to say, the pharmacist at the Dr. H. Bliss Murphy Cancer Clinic and I had a very close

---

1   Ivo Olivotto, M.D, The Intelligent Patient Guide to Breast Cancer, 175.

2   BC Cancer Agency CARE + AGENCY. (2013). For the Patient: Docetaxel injection.

telephone relationship during that time.

The other side effects of Taxotere included sore mouth, weak fingernails and toenails, and sores inside my nose. To protect my fingernails from possibly falling off, I had to soak the tops of my fingers, up to the first knuckle, in ice for the full hour of this particular treatment. Sounds like fun, hey? Taxotere is also the treatment that causes hair loss, numbing of the fingers, and tiredness.

The other chemotherapy I did was Carboplatin. This drug is known to cause nausea, vomiting, decrease in platelets, decrease in white blood cells, and tiredness. As perhaps other patients might agree, it's essential to keep focus as you endure the very troubling side effects. Yes, these are *not* the enemy; the cancer is! Yet, maintaining that perspective can be a challenge in itself.

These two chemotherapies continued for six treatments. I would go every three weeks and my day would last for about 5-6 hours. The first thing the nurse would do is hook me up to an IV (until I had my port put into my chest) and inject me with a drug called Emend. This was to decrease my risk for nausea and vomiting. That would run for half hour; then, we had to wait for a half hour for it to go through my system. Once that was in, they would start me on one of the two chemotherapies. When that was done I had to have a drug called Trastuzxumab which is also called Herceptin. This drug I would have to take for a full year. Herceptin *"is a monoclonal antibody, a type of protein designed to target and interfere with the growth of cancer cells."*[3]

When these cold liquids start flowing through your veins, you tend to get quite chilled. The nurses or someone attending with me would fetch me a warm blanket from the warmer. As

---

3 BC Cancer Agency CARE + AGENCY. (2014). For the Patient: Trastuzumab Herceptin.

well, my hubby made sure to always pack goodies like candies and snacks, not only for me but also for my many visitors!

Here is my first chemo Facebook post: *"2 am and I'm wide awake. Oh dear. My brain says "its Chemo day missus, get up!!!"*

So yeah, today is the Big Day. I get to put all the good advice to use; Mom's quilt is rolled up and ready to go to the hospital with me, slippers, hard candy, books, iPad for watching a movie, comfy clothes laid out...then I ask myself, "Is this really happening?" A little surreal I have to say.

So today I have to caution my sweet amazing circle of friends. As of today my white blood cell count will plummet to zero, nothing to fight anything with.

So, I welcome visits when I feel up to it but PLEASE, if you OR anyone close to you is sick, postpone your visit. I've been severely warned of this from friends who have walked this road AND my oncologist. I WILL end up in the hospital if I get even a little bit sick and Christmas is coming.

The support I have received so far is mind blowing, for myself, my family and my children. Some have said "I would have reached out but I didn't know what to say." Just saying that is enough, I'll take it from there. I have a way of putting people at ease, so no worries. NOT reaching out isn't the answer because I do miss you.

So lift one up for me today because I believe in a truly amazing God. He has moved mountains for me so far on this journey and I expect no less as I continue this walk through the valley. My hope and my faith is in Him, He will work through the amazing team of doctors I have, through my family and friends. Thank you for those who have truly stood by me, you know who you are. I continue to seek your love, prayers, and support.

#eternallyblessed #letskickthis!"

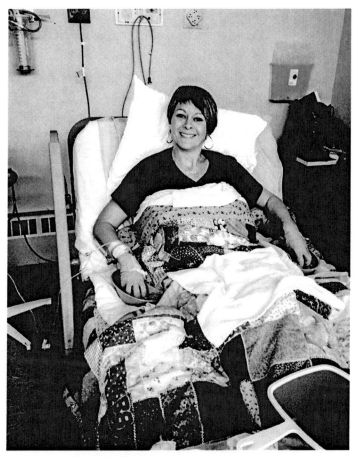

First Chemotherapy, November 19, 2015

I had to have an injection called Neulasta 24 hours after chemotherapy. This drug was to combat low white blood cell count, called neutropenia. Neutropenia increases your risk of infection. Of course, as with most drugs, there are side effects. The biggest one for me was crushing bone pain. I had the option of administering it to myself but the first time the nurse gave it to me, I began to faint. So I figured I had better play it safe and let the professionals do it.

I always had tons of visitors which helped me feel like I wasn't doing this alone. Their presence helped the time go much faster. My biggest supporters were my husband, my parents, my family, and my friend Sheila.

I would be remiss if I failed to send out kudos to the Dr. H. Bliss Murphy Cancer Center: they are truly amazing. Their staff, including doctors, nurses, maintenance, porters, administrative assistants, and volunteers, make the visit almost enjoyable. You nearly forget why you're there!

Chapter Ten

Faith in an Imperfect World

During my journey, many people would reach out to me in response to my regular Facebook posts. They would remind me of their prayers. Some would pass along quotes. On November 20th I shared this quote that had been sent to me: *"Faith sees the invisible, believes the unbelievable, and receives the impossible."* [1] I had made this my goal: to have faith and to foster my relationship with God, the One who sees way farther down the road than I can.

Many, many times along this path I have uttered the verse Jeremiah 29:11, "For I know the plans I have for you," declares the LORD, "plans to prosper you and not to harm you, plans to give you hope and a future." I have to say here that I don't profess to be perfect; far from it. I have made huge mistakes in my past. Some of these took years to forgive myself for. I felt the hurt I had caused others and shed many tears because of it. Still, through it all I was forgiven. I still had to live with the consequences of my bad choices, but God forgave me. It

---

1 McDaniel, Debbie. "40 Powerful Quotes from Corrie Ten Boom." Crosswalk.com, 21 May 2015, http://www.crosswalk.com/faith/spiritual-life/inspiring-quotes/40 powerful-quotes-from-corrie-ten-boom.html

wasn't until I could forgive myself that I truly accepted that.

The journey of cancer treatment also brought me to discard some of the things that were hindrances to faith. Growing up in a Christian home, we were taught about healing: "If it's the Lord's will then you'll be healed. If not, well, live with it." My incorrect conclusion through the years made me assume, then, that God was the source of illness.

In my 41 years I have learned a thing or two. I still don't know it all but I do know this: God didn't give me cancer. No, I believe this filthy man-made world gave me cancer. The pesticides, the pollution, the hormone- injected chicken and beef, and the boxed processed food might be the real culprits. And, let's not forget to add stress to that list. All these factors, combined with genetics, made me a prime candidate for the Big C.

What have I learned? Well, to do the opposite of course. That's what common sense would tell me to do: eat clean, grow my own food, stay away from processed foods, and avoid stress. Perhaps in a perfect world these would be possible. For the most part, I am making changes but I still have many competing realities.

I think the biggest culprit for me that set this cancer growing was stress. Far too often I let the garbage of other people's negativity affect me. I've heard myself and other people say "I can't help it; they make me so mad!" Well, I have to eat my words because, as I am learning, you CAN help it. Through prayer, meditation, relaxation techniques, and by surrounding myself with positive, uplifting people, I CAN change my reaction. I no longer have to accept other people's negative garbage. If they want it, they can have it. I however, refuse to take on other people's garbage.

During this journey I met with the Lymphedema Coordinator

at the Dr. H. Bliss Murphy Cancer Centre. She recommended a book to me: "100 Perks of Having Cancer" by Florence Strang and Susan Gonzalez. I had heard of this book from fellow cancer warriors so decided to see what the excitement was all about. I read through the chapters which I felt pertained to me. One particular section struck home to me. It reiterated exactly what I've felt all along. This is an excerpt from her book:

"Many books have been written about the mind-body connection: Love, Medicine and Miracles (Bernie Siegel, MD), The Power of Positive Thinking (Norman Vincent Peale), and You Can Heal Your Life (Louise Hay) are among my favorites. Both Siegel and Hay propose that cancer can be caused by underlying psychological factors. Hay says that cancer is caused by holding on to resentment, which eats away at the spirit as cancer eats away at the body. I think she has a good point. One of the questions that Dr. Siegel asks his patients is "What happened to you in the two years leading up to your diagnosis?" He believes that traumatic life events can serve as precursors to cancer. That makes sense to me. In the two years leading up to my diagnosis, I was under stress, and lots of it!" [2]

Let me share with you the events that confirm to me that stress was a major contributing factor. In the fall of 2014, an event occurred in my life and I was under a significant amount of stress. The littlest thing would send me into a spiral of tears and unexplained frustration. I could barely manage to put one foot in front of the other. Basic daily tasks became daunting to say the least. The last straw was when I walked into the porch one evening, saw that the mat on the floor wasn't straight, and burst into tears. I cried all the way into the washroom where my husband was taking a shower. Between sobs I said "The

---

2 Strang, Florence and Susan Gonzalez. "100 Perks of Having Cancer."

mat is squish". He said, "What?" Having no idea why this was bothering me so much made me cry even harder, "THE MAT IN THE PORCH IS SQUISH (my term for crooked)!" Well, that got his attention. He looked around the curtain, squinting so he wouldn't get shampoo in his eyes, and said, "Hon, I think it's time you go see a doctor."

I made a visit to my family doctor and naturopath who both took me off work and out of the gym. The results from the naturopath's tests showed that my whole adrenal system was flattened. My adrenal glands were wiped out, my iron was very low, my B12 was low, and I had zero zinc in my body (which aids in the absorption of iron.) Basically my "fight or flight" wasn't functioning. My naturopath was very caring and understanding and was a huge help in getting me back on my feet. This process took two months. I went back to work and the gym in January 2015. Nine months later I would be diagnosed with aggressive Stage 3 breast cancer. Good luck trying to convince me they're not related!

Maintaining faith in an imperfect world is still possible because of the God that has made unfailing promises to me. He is teaching me. Drawing me nearer. Showing me His ways. What was real at the onset of this journey is still holding me steady and bringing me forward.

Chapter Eleven

Be Strong - It's Only Hair

At the time I was diagnosed, my hair was down past my shoulder blades. Instead of taking the drastic leap from long hair to shaving my head, I decided to take it in baby steps. So on October 29th my hair stylist and very good friend cut it to a cute bob. Once I had a few weeks to get used to my neck being exposed and the light weight of having very little hair I decided it was time. November 22nd I had a "head shaving" party.

The thing is, when you're wading through something as personal and tumultuous as cancer, you deal with things in your own way, whatever that looks like. If people don't like it, too bad. This isn't about them, it's about you! I almost titled this book "IT'S NOT ABOUT YOU!"

Hubby and I invited my family and of course, my hair stylist Kayla. This was her first time shaving a cancer patient's head so it was a big event for her as well as for me. My brother Kerry came for support and decided he would humour us with Sinead O'Connor's song "Nothing Compares to U." We all got quite the chuckle out of that. It was tough, I won't lie. The only bright side to this was that some of it was dried up because of dyeing it and I needed a head of brand new hair... so it wasn't all bad!

There is a picture someone took while my hair stylist was shaving my head; I call it my "dealing" face. My eyes are closed; the hair is almost all gone. I see the look on my face and I remember thinking to myself, "Be brave, Denika, be strong. It's only hair. It's going to be ok." I had to believe that to keep going.

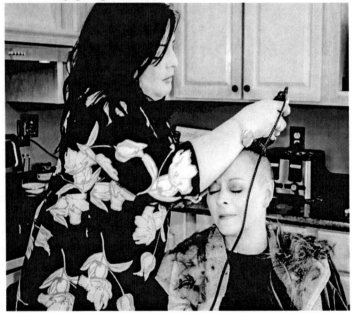

Kayla shaving my head with an electric razor.

The day of my head shaving Kayla posted this on Facebook: *"She stood in the storm and when the wind did not blow her way, she adjusted her sails."*

Denika Philpott, you became a client of mine many years ago that developed into a friendship I cherish very much. We have seen each other go through many ups and downs and when I didn't think you could inspire me more, you have.

Your positivity and attitude towards your cancer and certainty that will be beat is truly amazing.

I have always prided myself on looking my best (well most of the time.) I style my hair, apply makeup, and try and dress nice; so when you lose one of those things, your self-esteem takes a bit of a hit. But my husband never wavered. He would remind me daily that "he didn't fall in love with my hair." He would use humour and talk about how easy showers were now and how fast I could get ready. He was always looking for the positive. Thank you, Babe. You are my rock.

"A King always has his Queen's back."[1]

Some women who have lost their hair get fitted for a wig. Others choose to wear headscarves and some wear nothing at all to cover their bald head. For me, I chose to wear headscarves. I had a wide selection to match my outfits and it kind of felt like hair. Plus, my journey took me through the winter and I needed something to keep my head warm—so voila! I also had a couple friends knit warm hats for me. These came in handy on those freezing days trotting off to chemo!

On November 25th, I received a package in the mail. This was becoming a bit of a habit with people sending gifts, cards, and flowers. I opened it up to find a quilt that my sister Angela had ordered online. It came from Victoria's Quilts Canada. Their mission is to provide homemade quilts to people with cancer in Canada. My heart exploded when I realized how special this was. I cried like a baby. This became my "chemo quilt" as it came with a bag for carrying it so transporting everything I needed for chemo day became quite easy.

December 3rd I was scheduled to have a Portacath surgically

---

inserted into my upper chest (right side.) For those of you who don't know what a Portacath is, it's a chamber they insert under your skin on your chest wall which makes access to your vein for chemotherapy easier for you as well as for the nurses. This device also benefited me by saving my veins from being stuck over and over with needles. This was necessary for me because I was on Herceptin which is a *monoclonal antibody that interferes with the HER2 receptor and is used to treat certain breast cancers.*[2] This continued for a year. Not including biopsies, this was the first surgery I've ever had! Not bad for 41 years old.

As I lay on the gurney and the IV was placed into my vein, Darryl and I started chatting with the nurses. This team of nurses were super sweet and made me feel as relaxed as I could be considering what I was about to have done. One of their comments was pertaining to the doctor who would be performing my surgery. She said, "You're either going to get Vanilla or Chocolate." Perplexed I asked, "What?" She replied with, "There's two doctors who performs this surgery. We call one of them chocolate and the other vanilla. I'm not sure who's on today." When I looked, there was a Caucasian doctor shaking his head laughing. "Ohhhhh, I guess I'm getting the vanilla doctor today!" I said.

Once I was wheeled into the OR, I made sure the nurses all knew how nervous I was. I can just imagine what I looked like. I had only a bit of hair on my head, no make-up, face blotchy and this "Johnny gown" on that was about six sizes too big. Once I was settled on the table and they had given me some freezing, they started to make the incision. I yelled to the top of my lungs, "I CAN FEEL THAT!" The nurse laughed,

2   BC Cancer Agency CARE + AGENCY. (2014). For the Patient: Trastuzumab Herceptin.

"Ok, more freezing going in." All of a sudden I felt this total relaxation from the neck down. "Alright, I'm good; give 'er!"

During the surgery, Darryl was standing outside the door waiting for me. When it was over and they opened the doors, he said, "Were you guys having a party in there or what? All I could hear the whole time was all of you laughing your heads off!"

See? It's all in your perspective.

Chapter Twelve

Look Good, Feel Better [1]

By December 7th the tumour had gone from 14 x 15 centimeters before chemo to 8 x 10 with only one treatment done! What fantastic news! The oncology team were very pleased with how the tumour was responding to the chemotherapy.

As you can imagine, going through chemotherapy has a huge effect on your body in many ways. For me, I experienced nose bleeds and my hands turned completely red and then peeled from my wrist to my fingertips. Most of my body also peeled after chemo. My face became very blotchy with brown patches. I was trying very hard to use makeup to cover it up but I wasn't always successful. Then, knowing how difficult this was for me, my Mom signed me up for the "Look Good Feel Better" program which was hosted at the Dr. H. Bliss Murphy Cancer Center.

This program is a free, two-hour workshop which helps cancer patients learn how to look and feel like themselves again. *"Guided by experts through our Signature Steps, they master simple cosmetic techniques, explore hair alternatives, and learn about cosmetic hygiene, nail and skin care. Participants*

---

1 What is the Look Good Feel Better Program." http://lgfb.ca/en/

take home a complimentary kit of cosmetics and personal care products that are generously donated by the member companies of the CCFTA. The Look Good Feel Better workshop brings together women with cancer in a safe and supportive environment where they can share stories, insights, laughter, and yes, sometimes tears."[2] My experience was all that and more. I was chosen to be the hosts' model for different hair/ bald head techniques! What fun! For anyone about to go through the life-changing process that comes with cancer, call your nearest cancer clinic and they will connect you with the Look Good Feel Better workshop in your area.

"When you find yourself in the position to help someone, be happy and feel blessed because God is answering that person's prayer through you. Remember: our purpose on earth is not to get lost in the dark but to be a light to others, so that they may find their way through us."[3]

"What does having cancer teach you?" one might ask. Humility. During chemotherapy, you are stripped bare. It's because of this that when I came across this excerpt from "The Velveteen Rabbit," I completely broke. I unraveled at the seams. He said, *"You become. It takes a long time. That's why it doesn't happen often to people who break easily, or have sharp edges, or who have to be carefully kept. Generally, by the time you are real, most of your hair has been loved off, and your eyes drop out and you get loose in the joints and very shabby. But these things don't matter at all, because once you are Real you*

---

2 What is the Look Good Feel Better Program." http://lgfb.ca/en/

3 Ask Ideas. 29 March 2016. https://www.askideas.com/when-you-find-yourself-in-the-position-to-help-someone-be-happy-and-feel-blessed-because-god-is-answering-that-persons-prayer-through-you-remember-our-purpose-on-earth-is-not-to-get-lost-in-the-d/

can't be ugly, except to people who don't understand." [4]   This was so real to me and struck home so intensely to me that the tears are falling even as I am writing this. Anyone who has gone through or is going through a life-changing experience can appreciate this.

On December 10, 2015, I had my second chemotherapy treatment. Regarding the major issue of my hair, I already had my head shaved with an electric razor but I still had stubble. The following morning, December 11, I had a shower as usual. However, when I brought my hands down from my head while shampooing, I just stared in shock. It looked like I had placed my hands in dirt while they were wet. My two hands were full of this stubble. No matter how many times I ran my hands over my head, I would get the same result. There seemed to be no end to the stubble that was falling out!

After a half hour of cleaning the shower from these tiny hairs, I dried off, dressed, and called my husband in. "Hon, please, grab the razor blade, I can't deal with that again." Darryl did as I asked and slowly dragged his razor blade over my head, again and again, until all that stubble was gone.

My dog Kobi, who was such a faithful, loyal companion during my whole treatment regime, was very perplexed as to what was happening. He stayed by my side the whole time Darryl was shaving my head, watching as if he knew what this was all about.

You wouldn't think there'd be much difference in having stubble on your head and being completely bald, but there is. I felt 100% exposed and so very much like a cancer patient. From that point on I had to wear a sleeping cap at night because my

---

4   Williams, Margery. "The Velveteen Rabbit Quotes." Goodreads. https://www.goodreads.com/work/quotes/1602074-the-velveteen-rabbit

head was very sensitive. Even to lay my head on the pillow hurt.

Knowing this was only short term was a blessing. I looked forward to the day when my hair would grow back and I would no longer need head scarves, hats, head wraps, and night caps that made me look like "granny."

Darryl using a razor blade to shave my head.

Chapter Thirteen

Forward with

Deep-Settled Certainty

On December 22nd after celebrating my mother-in-law's birthday, this was my Facebook post: *"So to the list of foods I cannot eat: any kind of dairy, some veggies, fruit, spicy foods, and now I can safely add Chinese food.*

Had it for supper; now my stomach is convulsing and ripping itself apart...on top of that I get a nose bleed. It's not ALL glamour folks."

My brother is somewhat of an experimental cook at home. He loves to cook and is really good at it! His wife is often known to gift him with gourmet cooking classes which sound to me like a great night out. Once he learned about my dilemma with eating, he found a way to make one of my favorites and adapted it to my intolerances. Imagine having to make a cream-based soup, without cream! Well, he did it, and it was delicious. I pretty much lived off that for months.

On New Year's Eve I had my third chemotherapy treatment. My oncologist measured "the baby" (as my sister Michele and I had grown accustomed to calling the tumour) and it had shrunk to 4 x 5cms! Quite a decrease in size from 14 x 15 centimeters! Thank you, Lord!

We weren't sure what we were going to do for New Year's Eve. I usually throw a party for both our families but I was not in the position to do so this year. Friends of ours from church invited us to their house along with our church family. What a peaceful, amazing night we had! One of our friends said a prayer during the evening and with it a song settled on my heart: "Cover Me"[1] by Mark Condon. During his prayer, the peace that encompassed me was beyond understanding. Right then and there, I knew everything was going to be ok. I knew 2016 was going to be a hard year, but I had Him to lean on through it all. AND I will add that He has big plans for me. I know that because He told me so.

* * *

Being diagnosed with cancer changes more than just you; it changes the people around you. All of a sudden you and your partner have this DISEASE to contend with. The patient is trying to deal with a combination of not eating properly, lack of sleep, drugs being pushed into veins, pain killers, and anti-nausea meds. This is complicated further when the patient is not able to work. Normal functions of the body are gone out the window. Trust me when I say it makes for a somewhat stressful life.

My husband is great; he will go out of his way for anyone. But he's a male and as we all know, most males are "fixers." They want to fix everything. Therefore, at the beginning of this journey, we struggled. I felt he didn't understand me, and

---

1   Mark Condon. "Cover me." Online video clip. Youtube. Youtube.
     12 February 2012. Web. 30 November 2016.

he felt I didn't understand him. Thankfully, we had two sets of parents who have been married for many years who were very understanding and supportive.

After my third chemotherapy, and a somewhat heated discussion with my husband, I decided to go stay at my parents for a few days for both of us to gain some new perspective. This was soon after the Christmas season. Not only were we dealing with the stress from cancer and ALL that it entails, but also, neither of us were working. Through being open with each other, we both identified how we needed to work my sickness into our marriage. We also discussed how to cope with certain aspects of the challenge of the disease plus the side effects from the treatment.

> *"Be with someone who will take care of you.*
> *Not materialistically, but take care of your soul,*
> *your well-being, your heart, & everything that's you."[2]*

Chemo after chemo, the tumour was shrinking. By January 15 it was down to 4 centimeters x 4 centimeters! The oncology team was very impressed with the results they were getting. Again and again, they would marvel at how well I was responding to treatment.

During this time I felt the reassurance of knowing I was being taken care of. I knew I had an army of prayer warriors around me and they were praying without ceasing on my behalf. Gratitude filled me every time I would receive yet another victory report from my oncology team.

---

2 Took, L. https://www.pinterest.com/pin/158681586848809392/

Chapter Fourteen

My Parents, My Rock

For my parents, 2016 was a very rough year. My Mom spent weeks and weeks with me: cooking, cleaning, helping look after my children, and looking after ME! She wasn't a fan of driving in the winter, so she would hop aboard the DRL bus and make her way into Torbay where I live. Just knowing my Mom was there made it seem less unbearable. I can't count the number of times she would see me sitting on the couch rocking back and forth in constant motion trying to get the pain to subside. She would come over and start rubbing my legs just to see if it would help. Sometimes the noises of the house would end up getting to me so I would retreat to my sanctuary—my library. Mom would come in, sit in the other chair, and just be with me. This is an act of unconditional love that I will never forget and that I am truly thankful for.

I've always been "Daddy's Little Girl." As long as I can remember, if I ever wanted something, I'd go to Dad because I knew he always would say yes. As a parent myself, I can't imagine what it must be like to watch your child suffer through an illness. That feeling of helplessness must be brutal. During one week while recovering from chemotherapy, I went to spend a few days with my parents. The side effects from every chemotherapy treatment were different. This chemo, in particular, made me extremely nauseous to the point where I could barely turn my head. One evening while we were just hanging out and watching the news, I crawled over to the couch where my Dad was sitting and cuddled in. I truly felt like a sick 5-year-old needing her Daddy. How amazing it was to have the overwhelming support of my Mom and Dad throughout this year.

Being comforted by my Daddy

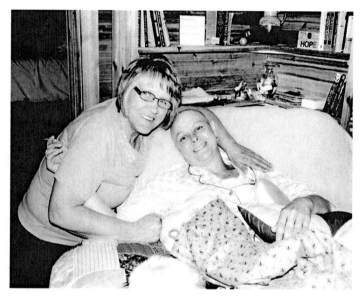

My hero and I.

"Sometimes all you need is for someone just to be there, even if they can't solve your problems. Just knowing there is someone who cares can make all the difference."[1]

* * *

I had so much encouragement during my journey. The messages I received were some of what kept me going. This post is from a lady from church: *"There is this woman I know; she is very brave. She is in a battle with the big "C" but man you would never say it. Her joy is radiant; her smile alone makes you feel everything is going to be alright. I hate cancer, but I love hearing about the victory. Denika, you inspire so*

---

1   Abney, M. https://www.pinterest.com/pin/470133648579195957/

many people, and your profile picture rocks!!"

I want to say again, "Thank you, from deep down in my heart, to all of you who made this very difficult journey a little easier."

Chapter Fifteen

One Step at a Time

Along this road I would only allow myself to deal with one aspect at a time. First it was chemotherapy. Ok, I had to learn about which chemo I would be taking, what its side effects were, how long they would last, how to deal emotionally, and how to stay sane through it all. So in January, I realized that March 3rd (my last chemo) would come quickly and any time after that I could be booked for my mastectomy. So, it was time to start researching the next big step. This was a giant step. This may be too much information for some people but I was an I-32. Yes, I was an I-cup; I'd be going from that size to less than flat. I say *"less than flat"* because my body is shaped in such a way that when they removed all the breast tissue, I was left concave.

Here is my Facebook post from January 20th: *"Just to let you know how real this journey is.*

I wouldn't allow myself to think about the (double if they'll let me) mastectomy I have to have after chemo until these past couple of weeks. But that time is coming closer and closer. As I started thinking about being rolled into the OR, taking one last look at "the girls", then waking up forever changed, I broke. Feeling totally unsure of how this surgery would change my life, the fear and uncertainty brought rivers of tears. I hugged into my husband crying: "I don't want this." Yes, most days are good, thank the good Lord, but, man, sometimes reality just slaps you right between the 2 eyes."

The January 28th Facebook post expresses more of those days of dire distress: *"Day 7 after my 4th chemo and wow, what a hit! I have been through the ringer this past week and I'm still not recovered. Very violent stomach cramping, bone pain that feels like people are beating me with baseball bats (I WISH that were an exaggeration), and nausea. Spoke with the cancer clinic pharmacist today and he has totally revamped all my "at home" meds. They are changing up my pain meds and my anti-nausea, as well as adding extra Dexamethasone (this is a steroid that helps protect my system from reactions.) I have been warned that the remaining 2 treatments are going to be much worse and I need your prayers, not only for me but for my family who are with me in this. Having said all that, I KNOW I will be "ok" but for right now, things are tough and this isn't fun."*

I pray to God that even through all of life's up and downs, that I will never become so bitter that I end up losing sight of what's really important: being *kind*.

> *"You either get bitter or you get better. It's that simple. You either take what has been dealt to you and allow it to make you a better person, or you allow it to tear you down. The choice does not belong to fate, it belongs to you.*[1]

A friend posted this on my Facebook during one of the worst chemotherapies: *"The enemy is not fighting you because you're*

---

1   "Bitter or Better." The Daily Quotes. http://thedailyquotes.com/bitter-or-better/

weak, he's fighting you because you're strong." These are the things that kept me going forward in a strong and positive way.

* * *

Most foods caused me tremendous pain. I relied mainly on bread and tea. And not just any bread; it had to be homemade bread. So, if I ran out of what people brought me, I would wait for the effects of chemo to wear off which usually took a week. Then the day I was feeling better, I would make a batch of homemade bread.

One morning about 6:45 a.m. as I was helping the kids get ready for school I started mixing my bread. This was about a week after a really terrible chemo. My son who was 13 years old at the time just looked at me shaking his head. I said, "What?" He said, "Mom, wow, just wow." I started to laugh. I said, "Well, Noah, when I'm sick I can't move. I can't do a thing. I can only lay around and wait to feel better. So once I feel better, that's it, look out, I have work to do!" My children have both seen me go through a lot this past year and I wonder how it has changed them. I'm hoping it has changed them in positive ways: to be more empathetic and less judgmental. And, through observing my family and friends, I'm hoping they learned what it is you do for someone when they need you. These caring actions have given them many examples of how to put their needs aside and focus on others.

"You never know how strong you are until being strong is the only choice you have."[2]

---

2 Wong, J "Lifestyle." Lifehack, Jelly Wong, http://www.lifehack. org/articles/lifestyle/you-never-know-how-strong-you are-until-being-strong-the-only-choice-you-have.html.

Chapter Sixteen

Sharing the Love

My son and daughter attend Youth at our church, Bethesda Pentecostal Church, located in St. John's, Newfoundland. On Valentine's Day as I was once again recouping from chemotherapy, I received a text from one of the young ladies from that group. She asked if I was home and if they could come by. What a surprise I got when 5 young people who represented Lytehouse Ministries showed up at my house bearing gifts! This beautiful bunch sat with me, laughed with me, and even prayed with me. What an act of true servitude.

This act of kindness prompted me to include a very important piece I wanted to make sure made its way into my book. From experience, I'd like to make a few suggestions about what to do for someone who is sick, or in my case, is home battling cancer. When you have a family, the preparation of meals doesn't stop just because Mom is sick. Life does go on and people need to eat. So, if you could organize a schedule with a group of friends to take turns providing the family with meals for the week after chemotherapy and for the next week to ten days, this would be a huge help! Even if you call in an order for pizza or a dinner from Mary Browns, it would be so appreciated. Over the months, we had a number of people deliver meals and even groceries. This was such a great help. We appreciated those acts of kindness so much.

The other way you can help is by finding out what the person uniquely likes, and bringing it to them. For me it was books and chocolates—which I was supplied with in great quantities! You could call his/her partner's cell phone or even ask their children what he/she enjoys.

Another possible expression of your caring concern could be to send money to help pay bills. Most often, the patient can't work or has to reduce the number of hours they work due to treatment. Even gas cards and grocery store gift cards graciously fill in the gaps. And, don't forget to include the children.

If at all possible, keep any and all stress away from the individual. Do not include them in drama that is unnecessary. Mind you, for me I wanted to help people. If one of my friends had a problem, I was the first to ask "What can I do?" That's just me. It made me feel like I still had a purpose, even if it was just to listen. What I'm talking about is causing undue stress, anxiety, or drama for the person going through an illness such as cancer. There's really no need to do so. And, in my opinion, stress grows cancer so it definitely won't be helping them.

If you're wondering about gifts, find out what the individual enjoys. Does that include any of the following: a journal to write her thoughts, scarf (for her head or neck), the Sparkles of Hope bracelet, make up, chocolates, candies, warm socks, slippers, the newest-released book, manicure, pedicure, or a massage. You could even do what a couple did for us: they took us out to dinner. What a fabulous idea! They waited until I was feeling up for it, made reservations, picked us up, and we had a lovely evening out. Don't think it has to be big and extravagant. It doesn't. Even a visit to sit and chat for a few minutes lets the person know you are thinking about them and means so very much.

Chapter Seventeen

Still Able to Laugh

When you have to take multiple medications for pain, for nausea, and then for bodily functions that are out of whack, your body kind of turns on you. I was never one to indulge in pills of any sort. Therefore, when I started taking all these medications along with the chemo still in my body, it took a bit of getting used to. Here is my Facebook post from February 18th: *"For those of you who have expressed your genuine care and concern, here is an update to post chemo #5 (it's been 1 week today.) The first couple of days weren't too bad. Mom came in to spend the week with me and I think her touch had a lot to do with how good I'm feeling; right Mom? However, the past few days have thrown me "in the weeds" as my hubby calls it. The bone pain became unbearable so I changed to a stronger pain medication. It took away the pain BUT caused excruciating stomach cramping/pain. Then last night I tried to get up and walk to my bedroom and I couldn't walk. My legs just would not support me! Needless to say, it was more than a little scary. Between Darryl and Mom, they carried me to the room and watched over me for about 2 hours until I was able to get up and go to bed. So thankful for Mom and Darryl. I seriously don't know what I would have done without them."*

In so much pain. The hard floor helped somewhat.

When you're in the middle of extreme pain, the silliest things strike you funny. As Darryl and Mom were lifting me up the step from my living room, Mom said, in a panic-stricken, high-pitched voice, "Do you have a chair with wheels on it? We'll roll her in the room!" I just started to laugh, "You're NOT rolling me around the house." Due to the fear of not being able to walk, the extreme stomach cramping, and the bent-over laughing, I barely made it to my bedroom.

See, even in the worst situations, there's room for humour.

* * *

One of my really dear friends wrote me the sweetest text message shortly before my last chemo treatment. *"I haven't told you in a long time, but Denika, you are amazing. You inspire me every day I look at your Facebook wall. You are pushing me to be a better me. Your fighting spirit is helping me walk a different journey with confidence. Someday I will share with you how your spirit and fight is impacting me in ways that you have no idea about. I know it hasn't always been easy to fight and be strong. There are days you just want to sit and cry but the way you bounce back from any obstacle this cancer throws at you is truly remarkable. Thank you from the bottom of my heart for being YOU and allowing your journey to change lives. I'm just one story. Over the course of time you will hear many, I'm sure, of how your journey and how you walked it impacted and changed their lives. February 2016, Denika Philpott is my hero. These are not just words and when the time is right I will share with you how."*

So wow! Talk about being floored! It's amazing how we can influence people (good or bad) and not even know it.

When you're going through the rigors of chemotherapy, you hurt all the time in one way or another. Your heart hurts, your ego hurts, and disappointment in people can cause you to hurt; yet, you look good. You make sure to always wear makeup. You cover your baldness with scarves or wigs. (And don't forget those big earrings that simply must be part of the "outfit!") You learn to cover your hurts well. So, for anyone you know who is wading through this terrible time in their lives, they need a hug. Don't hug too tight because the hurt is sometimes physical as well. But they need a genuine, long, and comfortable warm hug. Let them lean on you for those few minutes and feel the loving embrace of someone who truly cares. You'd be surprised at how much this helps.

"Scars are beautiful when we see them as glorious reminders that we courageously survived."[1]

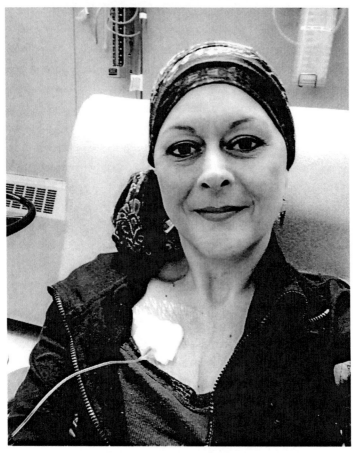

Get up, get dressed and get out.

---

1   Terkeurst, Lisa. Picture Quotes, http://www.picturequotes.com/
    scars-are-beautiful-when-we-see-them-as-glorious-reminders-that-
    we-courageously-survived-quote-487672

Chapter Eighteen

Surgery: Inside and Out

The day of my last chemotherapy treatment was such a memorable day for me. It became something I will never forget. At the Dr. H. Bliss Murphy Cancer Clinic they have established the "Bell of Hope." This bell rings very loudly so that the patients at the cancer clinic can hear it. The sound of that bell offers hope because it signifies the end of treatment. There is certainly cause for celebration whenever someone who has endured weeks of either chemotherapy or radiation finally completes their treatment. At times when chemo was the most severe I desperately longed for that bell to sound for my last treatment. The day finally arrived. I remember the feelings of relief and pure joy when I heard that sound and knew that I had reached a major milestone!

The bell was paid for by Newfoundland Power and the Dr. H. Bliss Murphy Cancer Care Foundation through their "The Power of Life Project."[1]

---

1   McLeod, James. "Davis gives emotional talk about cancer, unveils 'Bell of Hope'." The Telegram; Premier Paul Davis, Nikki Parrell. 8 May 2015, St. John's Nefoundland. http://www.thetelegram.com/News/Local/2015-05-08/article-4140812/Davis-gives-emotional-talk-about-cancer,-unveils-%26lsquo%3BBell-of-Hope%26rsquo%3B/1

Last chemo day. Two of my biggest supporters.

Team Denika

I have another funny story about my final day of chemo. Darryl, Noah, Abigail, and I made a "Last Chemo Day" sign. My friend and I were texting back and forth when we were drawing up the poster. Half way through I took a picture and sent it to her. Her response was "what's Las Cher Da mean?" Needless to say, the four of us cracked up laughing at this oversight. Didn't take her long to realize what the half-drawn sign would say when it was completed: Last Chemo Day.

* * *

After my last chemo, Darryl got called back to work. The miracle that he was off the months I had gone through chemo wasn't lost on either of us. On March 15th however, when I awoke to his side of the bed being empty, I burst into tears. I hauled myself up out of bed and went to visit friends. Later, I did some baking (therapy) and cleaned. Despite being kept busy, the reality of him going back to work and of me not working left me very lonely.

Leading up to my surgery was hard. I was trying to emotionally deal with the fact that I would be waking up with no breasts. As a well-endowed woman with an I-cup bra, waking up flatter than flat was tough to accept. Women may complain about their breasts but that doesn't mean we don't want ANY.

The day before my double mastectomy was a very emotional one. Darryl had to work in order to make sure he had enough days saved to take off during my surgery and recovery. Thus, his Mom accompanied me to pre-admission. We ran up and down the stairs for four hours in order for me to have an EKG, x-ray, and bloodwork. Plus, I had to meet with the physiotherapist I would be visiting after the surgery to discuss exercises. And then I'd be meeting with the anesthesiologist. While waiting for my results, someone whom I respect a great deal called me. After he told me his whole family were praying for me, he made a statement that I held onto during the really tough days. He said, "Denika, when I think of you and how you have fought this fight, I think, "She has the heart of a lion!" That really struck me as I thought about what others see. I know how I feel. I know that I make sure to always put my best foot forward when I go out, but for him to say that really impacted me. I knew I had to win this fight.

That afternoon as I arrived home, the reality of what was about to happen the next day hit me. The tears began and they just would not stop. I cried for hours and then cried myself to sleep.

On March 23rd I woke up, showered, and made my way to the hospital with Mom and Darryl. From the time I woke up until the time I went under anesthetic, I prayed for peace. "God, please go before me; please hold my hand as I fall asleep." I prayed for humour, so that when I was wheeled away from Mom and Darryl I wouldn't lose it. I prayed for my siblings who couldn't be there. I prayed for my Dad who was at home in Cottlesville tending to his "flock." Dad incubates and hatches hens, ducks, and quail. Unfortunately the hatching of baby chicks was happening at the same time as my surgery so he had to stay home.

I also prayed for my surgeon, asking God to guide her hands, and for the nurses. I lifted up my children before the Lord in prayer. I prayed for everyone who called, commented on my post, and visited.

My experience in the operating room was not what I had expected. Both Darryl and Mom had gone under anesthetic and offered comforting words to me about how well I would be treated in the O.R. Needless to say, this was not my experience. This was my first time going "under." I had only experienced biopsies before and for them I was awake. But, I had never had surgery before with the complete anesthesia resulting in me being "out." So, naturally I was scared. As I was wheeled in the O.R, I tried to joke with a nurse to still my nervousness. She looked at me, smiled, and then walked away. No one spoke to me! Of course, this made me even more nervous! Before I knew what was happening, both my arms were being strapped down to the bed out straight to my sides. I felt like a criminal on death row rather than a scared woman about to go through the biggest physical transformation of her life.

When I realized I was NOT going to receive any reassurance from the staff, under my breath I started to sing "No Longer a Slave" and by 10:00 a.m. the anesthesia had done its work and I was no longer awake.

During my surgery Mom and Darryl went to the cafeteria to get a coffee and wait. While they were standing in the line-up, thinking my surgery had already begun, Darryl turned around to see my surgeon standing behind him! With a very surprised look on his face he said, "Aren't you supposed to be doing surgery on my wife?" She laughed and said, "Yes, well, we're waiting for the anesthesiologist." Once that bit of information sunk in, he looked at her pleadingly and said, "You make sure you look after my wife." Mom piped up and in a nervous voice said, "Yes, that's my daughter in there." She assured them she would and walked away with her extra-large coffee. She was still holding that same cup of coffee when she walked toward them after the surgery was over.

I woke up in recovery at 1:30 p.m. and as my breast cancer friend suggested to me, started pumping the fist of my left hand to prevent lymphedema. With very groggy, slurred speech, I kept insisting that the nurse call my husband to let him and Mom know I was awake and doing well. Even though she told me over and over the doctor had already spoken to both of them, I wouldn't rest until I physically SAW her call him. I just didn't want them to worry any more than they had to.

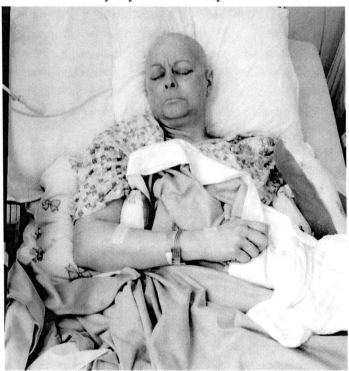

Sleeping after mastectomy surgery.

As I was wheeled into my room from the recovery unit, I was met by my Mom, Darryl, and my two first cousins. One of them had driven from Lewisporte (4 1/2 hours away from St. John's where I had the surgery) just to be with me. You talk about selfless! I did have pain when I got to my room but morphine and Tramacet helped alleviate that. That evening Darryl's Mom and Dad brought my children to see me along with Darryl's daughter. My brother's wife brought Mom and Darryl supper. What a thoughtful and practical gesture. Its things like that which help more than people even realize. After spending all day in the hospital they were quite hungry and that meal was much appreciated.

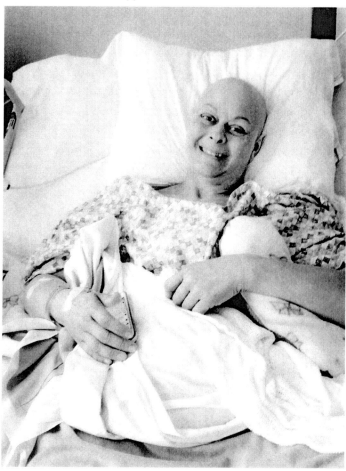

Wide awake after surgery.

"Trust that even in the twists and turns of life, God's in control. That's what faith is all about."[2]

2 Daystar.com. https://www.pinterest.com/pin/307652218275843706/

I went home at 10:30 a.m. the next day which I was very happy about. From the time I got home, I tried to alternate rest and some activity. After having a double mastectomy, the exercise routines are extremely important. The exercise routines prevent lymphedema and also assist you in regaining full movement of your arms.

The weeks following surgery were busy due to exercises, appointments, and healing. Mom stayed in with us and did my spring cleaning for me. She helped me empty my drain tubes and did a million other chores that had to get done. I don't know what I would have done without her during this time.

*Mom, Darryl and I out for a walk a couple days
after my double mastectomy.*

During my recovery at home my church Bethesda brought me a yummy fruit bouquet that all my family thoroughly enjoyed. The young adult group brought me a basket filled with homemade treats, candy, and snacks which I thought was the absolute sweetest gesture! I had a line-up of visitors from the time I woke up at the hospital and for days after.

It was during this time I was yet again disappointed in some who I thought were my friends. There were those people I had stood by for years that just dropped off the face of the earth. Thank God there were only a few. Nothing could feel worse than having people turn their back on you when you're literally fighting for your life. That hurt runs very deep. I had to focus on the amazing support system I had and to block those selfish people from my mind. If not, this journey would have been that much harder. I kept saying "not my garbage" and I was so much better off for it. A note in my journal during this difficult time said this: *"If you have a beef with someone, even if they ARE sick, it's better to confront them with it, resolve it, and move on rather than make excuses. When that person sees that you have time for everyone else except them, it's pretty clear."*

"I'm not interested in whether you've stood with the great. I'm interested in whether you've sat with the broken."[3]

My recovery time really brought back to the surface some disrupted relationships due to my past. Even before my surgery the Lord had been leading me to freedom and inner healing. The most important thing is to forgive—over and over and over. First of all forgive yourself and then others. For me, learning to forgive myself was a very tough struggle. I had made some really bad choices in the past that led to a lot of hurt and animosity. Accepting the consequences that came with

---

3 National Mill Dog Rescue. https://www.pinterest.com/pin/206673070379148192/

those bad decisions and then learning how to forgive myself were two of the hardest and most lengthy, painful processes I've ever been through. But it is so important so you can move on. Move past your mistakes, learn from them, and embrace the knowledge of your potential; God still has a plan for your life, even though you're not perfect.

In saying all this, if others decide to hold onto grudges (yes, it is a conscious decision) forgive them anyway. They are only hurting themselves—don't get caught up in them "not accepting" you or what they may say about you. The best tactic is to live your life honestly, with love, respect, and a heart full of forgiveness. Then their turned-up noses and lack of effort to move on won't bother you. My motto is "It's their loss."

"Not forgiving is like drinking rat poison and waiting for the rat to die"[4]

Yes, this was a time of surgery both inside and out!

Once I got home, the most challenging aspect of this surgery for me physically were the drain tubes. I had two coming out of my left side and one from my right. It was mostly because of these (and because of the pain) that I slept in my recliner in my library for the first few weeks.

Twelve days after my surgery, on April 5, 2016, this was my Facebook post: *I really don't know how to express my gratitude for my Mom. She basically moved in 2 weeks ago to help hubby look after me. He did a great job but then he had to go back to work. Without her, I would have been here alone, trying to look after the kids AND trying to recover from*

---

4   Lamott, Anne. "Quotable Quote." Goodreads,
    https://www.goodreads.com/quotes/39817-not-forgiving-is-like-
    drinking-rat-poison-and-then-waiting.

a double mastectomy...not to mention the effects of chemo still hanging on as well as the ongoing Herceptin. Mom, you have done so much for our family this past year. I don't know what to say that could ever repay you. I've seen the true meaning of "unconditional love" through you. Dad too...poor fella has been left to fend for himself. lol

Thanks SO much!"

Chapter Nineteen

Reason to Celebrate

I would be remiss if I did not mention a very important little baby: Jack. During the whole process of my diagnosis, chemotherapy, surgery, and everything, this baby made me smile so much, so many times.

Me cuddling Jack, my therapy baby

My diagnosis was October 8th and he was born October 27th. What a timely blessing! The joy he brought to my days can't be matched. As I review back over my Facebook page, it is sprinkled with pictures of me and this adorable baby boy. We were even actively engaged in a competition for hair growth! I want to thank his Mom and Dad for loving me through this journey and bringing their treasure to spend time with me.

Enjoying a beautiful day with Jack

On April 8th I returned to my surgeon for my pathology report. The trepidation and fear that lurked while waiting for her words almost choked me. Darryl and I sat waiting in the room at the hospital for what seemed like hours until she finally came. She was carrying a bulging file of paper—accumulated medical entries. While thumbing through it, her expression was one of "Oh!?" It was almost like she was surprised. My stomach rolled and my heart rate doubled. I had to ask, "What?!" She responded, "This almost never happens but you have *no cancer* remaining. There was scar tissue in your breast from the cancer and 6 out of 17 lymph nodes have scar tissue from them having cancer, but you're clear!" She was floored. It seems this is a rare occurrence, especially because the tumour I had was 14 x 15 centimeters before chemotherapy. In that moment, it felt like 100 pounds had been lifted off my shoulders. All of the painful process, the dread, and even the losses were worth it all. This "all clear" announcement was nothing short of a miracle and I thank God for it every day.

Five days later on April 13th I had an appointment with my oncologist to discuss my pathology report in depth. Once again, it was a time to celebrate the marvelous outcome. My Facebook post from the following day shared more of that celebration: *"I had a meeting with my oncologist yesterday. This amazing lady is real, honest, and super-caring. She is over the moon regarding my pathology report! It's squeaky clean, thank God! I do still have to go to the cancer clinic every three weeks for a year (this treatment is from Nov 2015-Nov 2016) to have Herceptin. This is an antibody which blocks the type of cancer I had called HER 2 from growing.*

The next immediate step for me is to start taking a pill called Tamoxifen. This pill blocks the action of estrogen (the cancer I had was estrogen-fed). I'm taking this particular pill because

I am considered pre-menopausal.

My oncologist is booking me for ovary removal surgery to rid my body of the biggest producer of estrogen. Then I will stop taking Tamoxifen and start taking an aromatase inhibitor (for post-menopause) which stops ANY and ALL production of estrogen. Ovary removal surgery will throw me head over heels into menopause. I will have to take this pill for 10 years.

Along with all this, radiation begins May 2nd, which is another new adventure for me. I'm researching it now so I can be "somewhat" prepared for how to treat my skin to minimize damage.

All in all, I'm feeling pretty happy these days. Chemo worked, I have a fantastic support system (you know who you are) and I am healthy!!! I embrace the good and expel the negative... AND I'm writing a book about my journey...yes the good AND the bad and I can't wait for you all to read it.

Lots of love xoxo"

As I read this now, I realize I didn't fully understand how Herceptin works and what HER2 meant. Let me explain using the resource of the internet:

"Genes contain the recipes for the various proteins a cell needs to stay healthy and function normally. Some genes and the proteins they make can influence how a breast cancer behaves and how it might respond to a specific treatment. Cancer cells from a tissue sample can be tested to see which genes are normal and abnormal. The proteins they make can also be tested. HER2 (human epidermal growth factor receptor 2) is one such gene that can play a role in the development of breast cancer.

The HER2 gene makes HER2 proteins. HER2 proteins are receptors on breast cells. Normally, HER2 receptors help control how a healthy breast cell grows, divides, and repairs itself. But in about 25% of breast cancers, the HER2 gene doesn't work correctly and makes too many copies of itself (known as HER2 gene amplification). All these extra HER2 genes tell breast cells to make too many HER2 receptors (HER2 protein overexpression). This makes breast cells grow and divide in an uncontrolled way."

This is where the treatment Herceptin comes in: *"Herceptin (chemical name: trastuzumab), which works against HER2-positive breast cancers by blocking the ability of the cancer cells to receive chemical signals that tell the cells to grow."*[1]

On April 14th, a good friend of mine and I went for lunch. I was only three weeks post-op but was bound and determined to get out of the house and enjoy some quality time with my friend. As we sat chatting she said something that gave me goosebumps. She said, "Denika, you know what I see when I look at you: I see a lion. Someone who has been faced with a challenge, who rises up in front of her family with her head held high and says bring it on." Remember the statement someone made to me during pre-admission? This was twice I was referred to as being likened to a lion. As soon as she said it I felt the power of God. This strength is not my own. Psalm 121:1-2 states the source to which I attribute the courage that they saw. "I lift up my eyes to the mountains—where does my help come from? My help comes from the Lord, the Maker of heaven and earth."

No matter how sick you may be or how much pain you are in, if you have children you have to get up and look after them. Thank God I was in between surgery and radiation when both my children ended up with the flu. And I mean full-blown influenza with high fevers, no appetite, and fatigue. I am so thankful it didn't happen during chemotherapy when my

1   "HER2 Status." BREASTCANCER.ORG, 29 September 2016, http://www.breastcancer.org/symptoms/diagnosis/her2.

immune system was super low. It was during their sickness though that I did have to have a minor surgery. On April 22nd I had to have a fair size skin tag removed from my mastectomy site. Four stitches later I was ready to get back to the house and nurse my darlings back to health.

"Never will I leave you; never will I forsake you"
Hebrews 13:5

"I took you from the ends of the earth, from its farthest corners I called you. I said, 'You are my servant'; I have chosen you and have not rejected you. So do not fear, for I am with you; do not be dismayed, for I am your God. I will strengthen you and help you; I will uphold you with my righteous right hand."
Isaiah 41:9-10

Chapter Twenty

Sustained by Love

Just nine weeks after the mastectomy, on May 9, 2016, I began the first of the 25 radiation treatments. My Facebook post for that day shares the account: *"First radiation done. All the while lying on that bed I was singing Chris Tomlin's song "Whom Shall I Fear (God of Angel Armies) ... "nothing formed against me shall stand, you hold the whole world in your hands, I'm holding on to Your promises, You are faithful, You are faithful...."* [1]

During chemotherapy and Herceptin, I had a choice to either sit in a comfy chair or lie in a hospital bed if I felt tired or unwell that day. And, during the previous chemo treatments, I would have heated blankets wrapped around me with my family and friends surrounding me for support. Radiation is quite the opposite; no comfortable chairs or beds, no heated blankets, and no one to offer me comfort and reassurance. I wasn't sure what to expect and truthfully, I was nervous. Once I went into the room and lay on the bed, I was even more scared and fought the urge to cry. In that room, lying on a hard bed with

1   Gonzalez, Angela. Kim, Payton. Janis. Scharstein, Rob. Lothamer, Jennifer. "Whom Shall I Fear (God Of Angel Armies)." AZ, http://www.azlyrics.com/lyrics/christomlin/ whomshallifeargodofangelarmies.html.

my body tugged and twisted so the markings line up properly, and with a huge rumbling machine orbiting around me, I was petrified. Because I have scoliosis, my body is curved and twisted so the team would have to tug my hip one way, then push my left shoulder down. And on and on it went until I was "in position." I would then end up in excruciating pain for the duration of the treatment. I sang every hymn, chorus, or song I could think of. Of course, while being strapped onto the bed, I wasn't allowed to move a muscle which made the whole thing that much more daunting.

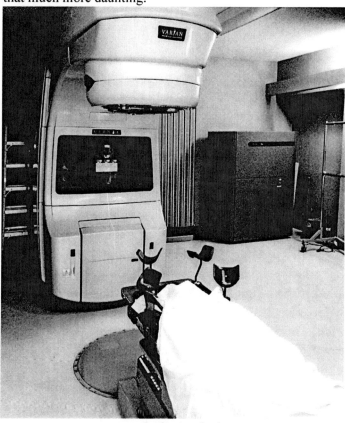

Radiation bed.

I would like to say I got used to it, that it became less scary, and I didn't mind it but, I'd be lying. I was terrified of being alone with the radiation machine doing its thing. However, the songs from my playlist kept running through my mind and I would sing them constantly and pray. 1 Thessalonians 5:15-16 became so real to me during all 25 treatments: *"Rejoice always, pray without ceasing, give thanks in all circumstances; for this is the will of God in Christ Jesus for you."* The part of the verse I've underlined was the part I practiced daily. This was a constant communion with God. During one of the treatments I felt Him standing behind me with His arms wrapped around me. At once I felt peace and experienced a warm presence that literally made me 100% relaxed. The Presence of the Lord by His Spirit is such an amazing, supernatural phenomenon that we often take for granted. What a wonder it is to have the power of the Holy Spirit come to where we are and comfort us. Thank God for His presence.

The May 16th Facebook post expresses some of this challenge: *"You ever feel like crying, just because?? For gratitude, for learning through pain, for being stretched at the hand of God, for giving yourself over 100% to His plan.*

This year has been very humbling and empowering (I know they sound like opposite things and that's ok. If you know me and my story, or can relate to this, you'll know what I mean.)"

Anyone who has gone through a struggle, whether it is cancer or really any such challenging experience, knows what I meant by that post. A lot of the time, we may feel like WE are in control. WE know what's best for our lives, WE know which decision is the right one and WE have all the say. Well, I've learned that is not the case. For me, when I've taken matters into my own hands, the end result is always catastrophe, utter chaos, and hurt. I believe God has really shown me a lot this past year. I've experienced being humbled like I never would have had if I not trudged on through this journey. I've gained understanding for those who suffer. I've had a glimpse into what selfish and selflessness look like. And, I've established a connection with my Father in heaven that I never experienced before.

Every morning during my "getting ready" ritual, I would listen to my playlist. The tears would roll down my cheeks and I would talk to God. It was during these quiet times that He would speak to me. I would experience His Presence flooding into my spirit. I would be overwhelmed with His grace and love

Yes, I was experiencing so many new things from His attending Presence. Yet, this was happening in the midst of continuous challenge. This is from the May 24th Facebook post: *"#11 and counting.*

Had a great weekend celebrating my niece's wedding... beautiful all around.

Bit of a tough go personally though...the "no hair, no 'shape'" was a hit to my self-esteem. Looking at pictures of myself amongst beautified, gorgeous-haired, curvy females affected me in an intimate way that only people who've undergone a physical transformation will understand. It may sound vain, and I don't mean to be, it's more of trying to accept my "new normal." All a part of this journey I guess."

To some people this may sound vain and a little petty; but, I will try to express what this actually feels like: I've lost a big part of me. When you go through chemotherapy, your skin changes. Mine became blotchy with parts of my face white and the other brown. Then you lose your hair and underneath all that hair was a not-very-attractive, gleaming white scalp. After surgery, you expect to be "flat chested." This wasn't the case for me. I ended up with a very pronounced chest wall now sloping backward on each side where once my breasts had been. Needless to say, nothing fit right. And, at this point, I was so sore from radiation that even when I would wear a little padded bra it felt like I was wearing jagged wire.

As a young girl and into young adulthood I suffered from low self-esteem. I have my theories about why, but I won't go into that here. As I got a little older and grew into myself, that low self-esteem got a little better but never to where it should have been. Then I'm thrown into the biggest physical transformation of my life. I say to myself, "Denika, you are so fortunate to be alive!" I know I am blessed. I know others who have not been this fortunate. Yet I still have to learn to live with this "new me." I cannot let lack of breasts or scars or 1-inch hair define who I am. This is tough in a society that lives and breathes air-brushed models and curves. This is an ongoing battle for me. It is one that I will win with the help of my husband, my parents, friends, and my amazing Lord.

On June 1st the trauma of the past 8 months grabbed a hold of me and threatened to sink me. Never in my life had I ever felt so lost, alone, and in utter despair. I tried to shake it off by going shopping, but the darkness that tugged at me was stronger than even the remedy of shopping! I pulled into the Canadian Tire parking lot to head in to look for a Father's Day gift for Darryl, but I couldn't even get out of the car. The tears just would not stop. My chest heaved and I cried harder than I had in months. I was texting with one of my good friends. I am forever thankful for her because she understands me in a way no one else does. At that moment, Darryl texted to ask me how I was. I replied with something like "Not good." Of course, he was working but took the time to call me and see what was going on. We chatted through my sobs but on that particular day nothing anyone said was going to help me feel better. I was in a very dark, cold place and had to figure out a way to get out. I hung up from him and really struggled to get control. I said to myself, "Ok, Denika, stop. What would you do now if you knew no one would judge you? What do you need to make yourself feel better?" And in that moment, I knew. Once I had stifled my sobs, I drove home and got in my Jacuzzi that hubby had so thoughtfully installed in my library. Once I relaxed for a bit, I curled up in my daughter's bed, poured up a full glass of wine, watched one of my favorite movies (*Eat, Pray, Love*[2]) and ate Miss Vickie's chips and mini eggs.

After the movie was over, wine gone, chips and mini eggs devoured, I felt a tiny bit better. Yet, that evening was really tough and the dark cloud did not really lift. Only temporary relief came in my rather feeble attempt to break the grip. Even though people may try to enter into your feelings and understand what you're going through, they can't. So that night rolled along like any other; homework, supper, dishes, etc. All the while I was hollow, lonely, and scared. Being in that pit, I tell you, is not a fun place to be. In fact, it was downright scary but I knew it was up to me to crawl back out. I was determined to do whatever it took to get back on solid ground.

The next day I painted on my favorite lipstick, donned my new shirt, and went to Starbucks to engross myself with other people and my favorite thing, books. While I was sitting there, I received a call from a friend of mine. She wanted to tell me about a lady she knew who had met me at the cancer clinic the week before while I was having Herceptin. When the lady had started to tell my friend about "the lovely lady" she had met at the cancer clinic my friend realized she was talking about me! She said "I HAD to call and tell you all the nice things she

---

2 Eat, Pray, Love, dir. by Ryan Murphy (2010; Columbia Pictures Industries, Inc.2010 DVD)

was saying. You DO impact people without even knowing it."

Yes, I remembered sitting across from this very sophisticated woman who was waiting to see if she could have chemotherapy that day. Her sister was sitting with her and as I finished up and was leaving, she spoke to me. She started to tell me how beautiful and strong she thought I was. A couple of days later, I bumped into her at a grocery store and she said the same things again.

What a blessing after the week I had! I now realize that the "dark place" I was pitched down into was a stage of grieving. I had indeed experienced losses through the entire ordeal of the cancer. When it all seemed to catch up with me, I couldn't rise above it by myself. In the gracious way of the Lord, He allowed the report to come back to me at just the right moment. The response of that lady I had met was a mirror to me of who I really was because of the gracious work and sustaining of the Lord. His timing plus that feedback became another tender expression of His sustaining love for me. All of that broke the grip of the dark shadow. The Lord works in mysterious ways to confirm His love to us!

Chapter Twenty One

More Changes Still

On May 26, 2016, I had an appointment with my gynecologist to discuss my ovary removal surgery. However, a surprise awaited me. I was to learn that I was actually scheduled for a compete hysterectomy! Of course, this surgery would immediately put me into menopause. I would start an aromatase inhibitor which works by reducing the total amount of estrogen in the body. It actually starves cancer cells by depriving them of estrogen.

My Facebook post shares how I was processing this startling news: *"I've just learned that I'm booked for surgery July 4th for a complete hysterectomy. The ovaries I knew were coming out because we need to stop the production of estrogen to lessen my chances of reoccurrence. (This is because of the type of cancer I had, HER2, ER positive.) But this decision to have a full hysterectomy is news to me. My OB-GYN is afraid if we leave the uterus, I may end up with endometrial cancer down the road so...out she comes.*

Did I cry? Yes

Am I tired? Yes.

Do I want this to be over? Yes.

But I'll keep trucking along...looking for the good in things, enjoying my family, my friends and all the little things.

Only the Lord Himself knows where all this is going to lead so I'm trusting Him to bring me somewhere after this that will glorify Him."

Once the date was set I made a phone call to my oncologist to keep her up to speed. I assumed she may not know about the decision announced to me by the gynecologist. When I told her the date she said I had to change it because Herceptin is due just 3 days later. After going through such an extensive surgery, I wouldn't be up to having the Herceptin process. And postponing the Herceptin was not an option. (Remember, this is the ongoing treatment I was to have for a full year, Nov 2015-Nov 2016.) As a result, a new date for surgery was set: July 18th. The hysterectomy would be another mountain to climb, but a necessary one nonetheless.

* * *

While awaiting the compete hysterectomy, my radiation treatments continued. With the type of radiation I had, I had to go every weekday. I had Saturday and Sunday off. At first the weekends off didn't mean a whole lot to me; however, toward the end, it was such a blessing. There are different reactions among those who have radiation. Some burn with the treatment, others don't. Well, I was one of the unfortunate ones that burned, badly.

After my mastectomy I had to have physiotherapy on my chest wall so that the scar tissue would "unstick" and help with overall healing. It was during my second last visit that my mastectomy incision started to seep due to the excessive pushing on my tender skin. I know what you're thinking, gross! And it was, not to mention the steps I then had to take to heal that spot. Another round of radiation loomed around the corner. It took the combined efforts of the radiation doctor, my family doctor, and the community health nurse to slowly get the damaged area to heal. However, because of the length of time it took to achieve that progress, the radiation scheduled for May 2nd had to be postponed until May 9th.

Finally, radiation was over on June 13th and not a day too soon! Upon removing my gown for my last treatment, the radiologist said "You had better apply some cream to your top left shoulder/back when you're done." The radiation had gone right through.

The pain I experienced over the following weeks is hard to explain. Anyone who has had severe burns can relate. It's intense pain from the inside out. The lovely community health nurse was a God-send to me. She directed me to obtain a prescription for Flamazine (used to treat and prevent infection) as well as hydrocortisone cream for the continuous itching I experienced. She would apply Mepitel (mesh, non-stick layer) over the severely burned areas, cover that with a gauze (NO TAPE) and then wrap my body from the waist up with a mesh to hold everything in place. I stress "no tape" because no adherent was to be used on the whole radiation area due to the skin being so weak and thin. Pulling tape off would surely bring skin with it.

Along with hot flashes due to early onset menopause from the drug Tamoxifen, I was now in the middle of summer, wrapped in gauze, mesh, and slathered in Vaseline for hydration purposes. "Uncomfortable" doesn't even come close to describe how it felt. Sleep would have been impossible if not for a sleep aid.

> *"God doesn't give the hardest battles to the strongest women; He creates strong women through life's hardest battles."[1]*

1   "To the Guy that Made Me Ashamed of Myself." brinicolesays, 15 June 2016, https://brinicolesays.wordpress.com/

Once the burns had healed and the pain had subsided, I had to gear up for yet another surgery: a complete hysterectomy; uterus, ovaries, fallopian tubes and cervix. My gynecologist wanted to eliminate any chance of female cancer recurrence.

I was scheduled for surgery July 18th at 9 a.m. Darryl, Mom and I arrived at the hospital at 7 a.m. for the preliminary procedures that happen before every surgery. At 9 a.m. I walked into the operating room and lay on the table, all the while thinking back to the terrible experience I had when I had my double mastectomy. However, thank God, this time was very different. The nurses were friendly and the surgeon even sat with me before I went into the OR to clarify any questions, doubts, or concerns I may have had. I appreciate that gesture more than she will ever know.

Before I knew it I was back in the room, unable to keep my eyes open. I remember nothing of the recovery room or my ride up to my room. Of course, Darryl and Mom were with me the whole day as I slipped in and out of a very groggy state.

My Mom recounts that for both of my surgeries, seeing me for the first time as I was being wheeled to my room was the worst. Having experienced breast cancer at the age of 52, this brought back a flood of memories for my Mom. I guess for her, thinking that her baby had to journey this long road ahead, was hard. When you're sitting on the sidelines watching someone you love go through what I have been through this year, it can get really tough. I am so thankful for the multitude of friends my Mom and Dad have. All through this journey they were always there to comfort and pray with them, making sure they checked in to see how they were holding up.

"Watching someone you love suffer is sometimes worse than suffering yourself."[2]

For the weeks following my hysterectomy, I was instructed to rest in a reclined position for the first three weeks. Then I could slowly get back into walking and moving around. I was to do no lifting, cleaning, or activity of any kind for six weeks. The first week I stayed home in Torbay and my Mom and hubby looked after me. Then my Mom, my children, and I went out to my hometown where I grew up to recuperate. My husband joined us for the last few days so he could drive us back to Torbay where we live. Not doing anything was HARD! It was tough to not dust, to notice things out of place, or to see plants that needed to be watered and not be able to do anything. Thankfully my children were very helpful and did anything I asked them to do. Once we were back home in Torbay, Mr. & Mrs. Pike, my husband's parents who live with us, were always there to help out in any way they could.

---

2 "Sizzle." Halos and Horns, 25 September 2016, https://onsizzle.com /i/watching-someone-you-love-suffer-is-sometimes-worse-than-suffering-2540604.

Chapter Twenty Two

The New Normal

People continue to say "Sure, you're almost back to normal." I know they mean this to comfort me and bring to me some sense of "everything is going to be ok." In actual fact, I feel nothing will ever be "normal" again.

So, let's be real for a moment. In the immediate weeks right after my mastectomy I didn't feel that losing my breasts was a big loss. I didn't feel like I had become the monster that I had imagined. I was pretty ok with it. However, as time crept on and I found myself in certain situations, it bothered me more and more. My sexuality took a severe beating. The feeling of femininity and that feeling of "I look good" had all but vanished.

When you're being intimate, how do you deal with this new body? For me, my breasts were a package deal with intimacy in our bedroom. I vividly recall the conversations I had with myself trying to adjust. "Now, they're gone. But even deeper than that, I am scarred. As a result of the radiation, I am burned. As an ex-I cup, sexy (my own feelings of myself) female, how do I deal with now being but a scooped-out, scarred version of the old me? In our times of intimacy do I remain covered from the waist up? Do I just pretend it doesn't bother me? Do I use humour to cover it up? Should I buy a padded sexy bra and pretend they're still there?" It's a struggle, it really is.

What and who I am now is an evolving person with fragments of who I used to be. The awkward shape of my chest reminds me daily that I am far from "normal," or in my words, far from the "old me." The memories of my journey through this year fighting cancer and the feelings they conjure up remind me that I am no longer who I used to be. In addition to the other changes, I now struggle daily with immediate onset menopause which is medically proven to be twenty times harder on women than the slower, natural process.

My goal is to work toward being confident in spite of my new body, of my scars, and what I no longer have. Through my book and sharing with other people, I want to be able to help those who are going through a rough time whether it be with cancer or some other struggle in their lives.

I thank the Lord daily for my life and for my health and strength. I thank Him that I am able to put two feet on the floor every morning, get myself dressed, and look after my family.

God is good, folks. I know He didn't give me cancer but I do know He took this past year and weaved it into His plans for me. I sense His plans for me are going to blow my mind; I can expect great things that will glorify Him. I'm so excited to see what's in store for me and I hope you will join me as I continue on my journey.

"When you stand and share your story in an empowering way, your story will heal you and your story will heal somebody else."[1]

---

1 Vanzant, Iyanla. "Quotable Quote." Goodreads, https://www.goodreads.com/quotes/698887-when-you-stand-and-share-your-story-in-an-empowering.

My hubby Darryl and I

My darlings kiddies, Abigail, Noah, and I

Chapter Twenty Three

One Year Later

A few years ago I told someone I would stand in front of a group of people and tell my story. At the time I had no idea what that talk would be about. Fast forward a couple of years and I've been diagnosed with cancer and have endured rigorous treatments and radical surgeries. I have written a book, have started a new business, and have been invited to speak at a retreat and model clothes at a women's event. How God can take a mess and transform it into a message is just one more miracle I have been blessed to experience.

Walking through the journey of cancer and the unknown, waiting for test results, having to fight for someone to take me seriously, plus the diagnosis, chemotherapy, double mastectomy, radiation, a complete hysterectomy and Herceptin—all this opened my eyes to so much!

When you experience an extreme change in every aspect of your being, you have to develop a new acceptance of yourself. I still like to look nice. I have a healthy dose of self-love and self-respect. After I had all the treatments and surgeries, I was left with a new me. I was left with the question, "What makes Denika, Denika?" The answer to that would be not what other people think I am but what I know I am.

I am made in the image of Him, my amazing Lord. He is the One who held me in the palm of His Hand as I sat in misery on the floor of the bathroom, the One who wrapped His arms around me lying on the bed receiving radiation, and the One who held my hand while I had my surgeries. He never left me nor did He forsake me. I love Him and I love the person I am today. I have gone through so much and it has made me the person I am.

I have learned that we all have a purpose. Sometimes that's hard to believe about ourselves, but it's so true. There have been times I doubted my purpose—but then I seek God and ask Him to intervene. I surround myself with positive people. And I open myself up for the plan God has for me. I can now declare with confidence: trust Him. It will come.

Cancer took a lot from me: opportunities, my breasts, my whole reproductive system, self-worth, time, and believe it or not, people. Yet I gained so much! I learned what it means to be humble. I learned a compassion I never knew. And I learned to rely totally on the Creator.

Now, one year later I am writing a book. I have started a new business as a TPI Travel Consultant. I am involved with public speaking about my journey. I have built amazing relationships with some very special people. And I know God isn't finished with me yet!

* * *

The title Overcomer seems like a very fitting title for someone who just beat cancer. On November 15, 2015, 4 days before I started chemotherapy, my very good friend Tammy Tetford came to visit me. During her visit she gave me a beautiful Willow Tree ornament and a necklace. The necklace has a little name plate on it and engraved on it was the word *Overcomer*. When I looked at that word, I realized how much faith I was going to need until I could claim that I was indeed an *Overcomer*. Little did I know then that I would write a book and name it that powerful title.

My good friend Tammy & I
(I'm wearing the Overcomer necklace)

* * *

Me before cancer, July 2014

Me after cancer, September 2015

I had my last Herceptin, November 10, 2016. I know my journey isn't over yet and there's more to come. I am trusting my Heavenly Father to lead the way and guide me to share my story of victory through Him. My story gives hope and encouragement that you, too, can overcome whatever life throws at you.

About the Author

Denika Philpott

Photo Credit: Wanda (Cooze) Stead

Denika Philpott is a vibrant and passionate individual whose story will inspire you. For the past year, Denika has been fighting for her life with the Big C. She was diagnosed with aggressive Stage 3 breast cancer on October 8, 2015. Since then Denika has waded through the murky waters of chemotherapy, a double mastectomy, radiation, and a complete hysterectomy. Yet, here she is, still lighting up rooms.

Denika worked as a Sign Language Interpreter for 16 years and is now pouring her passion into writing and her love of travel as a TPI Travel Consultant.

She is a mom of two amazing children, Noah (14) and Abigail (12), and a furry companion who stole her heart five years ago, Kobi. She is also a friend to her husband's three adult children. Denika, her husband Darryl, and their children live in Torbay, Newfoundland Labrador.

Stay Connected

Denika would like to stay connected with you as she reaches each milestone and each victory on this journey.

Visit https://journeywithdenika.wordpress.com/ to keep up to date on her journey as an Overcomer.

Visit Denika's TPI Travel Consultant webpage to book your next vacation. On her webpage you will find pictures of the different places Darryl and Denika have explored. Now, let her help you plan that trip you've always dreamed about. http://tpi.ca/DenikaPhilpottTPI/

Also join Denika's TPI Travel Consultant business Facebook page: https://www.facebook.com/denikalynnphilpott/

Email Denika directly at denikaphilpott@yahoo.ca

CPSIA information can be obtained
at www.ICGtesting.com
Printed in the USA
LVOW08s0142140117
520949LV00001B/1/P